Archaeological Guides

General Editor: GLYN DANIEL

Sicily Margaret Guido
Southern Greece Robert and Kathleen Cook
Denmark Elisabeth Munksgaard
Malta David Trump
Persia Sylvia A. Matheson
Central Italy R. F. Paget
Southern Italy Margaret Guido
Southern England James Dyer

WALES:
An Archaeological Guide

Wales:
An Archaeological Guide

*the prehistoric, Roman and early
medieval field monuments.*

CHRISTOPHER HOULDER

FABER AND FABER LIMITED
3 Queen Square London

First published in 1974
by Faber and Faber Limited
3 Queen Square London WC1
Printed in Great Britain by
Alden and Mowbray Ltd
at the Alden Press, Oxford

ISBN 0 571 08221 1

TO

all those who have recorded the archaeological heritage of Wales, sometimes inaccurately, often with lively imagination, almost always with complete integrity of purpose. From their writings these pages have been compiled for the guidance of others who come to enjoy that heritage and to contribute in their turn.

CONTENTS

ACKNOWLEDGEMENTS

In addition to the acknowledgements below, I would like to thank especially the Royal Commission on Ancient Monuments (Wales) for unrestricted access to records and maps; and in general the staff and honorary officers of museums, university departments and government offices throughout Wales for helpful suggestions and comments.

Permission to reproduce copyright material is gratefully acknowledged. Sources are indicated in the captions of Plates. Aerial photographs by Prof. J. K. S. St. Joseph are in the Cambridge University collection. Most of the line drawings have been made by Mr Dylan Roberts, any variation from originals being the responsibility of the author. Originators are indicated in the captions of Figures. Figs. 4, 16, 19, 29, 31, 34, 35, 36 are taken from photographs published or supplied.

Christopher Houlder
Bryn-llwyd,
Cliff Terrace,
Aberystwyth,
Dyfed

ILLUSTRATIONS

PLATES

ILLUSTRATIONS

FIGURES

FOREWORD

Some explanation is needed of the arrangement of this book and of the scope of the information contained in it, which have been influenced by certain basic assumptions:

1. In a land that has been robbed of most of its railways, and where bus services are irregular, the normal means of travel is the private motor vehicle; territorial subdivisions and the length of suggested circuits have been determined accordingly for motoring convenience.

2. The tourist who is sound in wind and limb is willing to use both within the normal limits of effort and in all reasonable climate and terrain. The less fortunate reader should be able to visit many of the sites described, since the nearness of passable roads has been considered in their selection.

3. Good maps will be ready to hand for use in conjunction with the book. The Ordnance Survey 1:50,000 series is the widely accepted standard, on which almost all the recommended sites are marked.

Finding and Approaching Sites

A guide of wide coverage cannot give the location of sites with great precision, nor can the best approach be described in detail. The text remains silent in all matters which are subject to change, such as land ownership, rights of way and natural conditions, and it is left to the individual user of the book to reach a site by a combination of map-reading and an 'eye for country'. One unpredictable factor is the countryman's reception of the unexpected visitor, for though a farmer may have a friendly attitude about access to the antiquities on his land, the lambing season or a hay crop may be the cause of some reluctance. This is a matter of personal diplomacy, in which one's absorption in the past is at least a reasonable motive. In the wilder mountain areas no question arises, but enclosed land is best approached through the nearest farmyard. At a time when vandalism and urban encroachment are increasing the countryman's suspicion of strangers, any attempt to take a quick look unobserved entails the risk of wrong identification as a poacher or a planner, and of spoiling the chances of those who come later.

The descriptive material is arranged for ease of reference rather than for continuity, which can be obtained from the introductory Outline (p. 31) and from some of the books listed in the Bibliography (p. 194). The eight regions which are presented as separate chapters are further divided into a total of 45 *areas* to provide convenient tours. These have been numbered and distinctively named, as shown on Fig. 2 (pp. 22–3).

The sectional heading for each area contains basic information for planning a day's outing:

Length of tours. Few tours involve more than 100 kilometres (62 miles) of motoring, or more than 8 *primary sites* to visit. The longest are better divided if time allows, while the shortest can be made to last a whole day or can be combined with other areas. *Secondary sites* can be included as convenient. The organisation of the information is thus intended to be helpful and not restrictive.

Maps. Wales is covered by 23 maps in the Ordnance Survey's latest series (1 : 50,000). The greater detail of the o.s. $2\frac{1}{2}$-inch series (1 : 25,000), though more useful for reaching sites, comes expensive at only one-sixth of the coverage. The indication of rights of way is now virtually complete at the larger scale, which has replaced the one-inch series, (1 : 63,360).

Counties. To assist in reference to the literature, the traditional counties within which the sites lie are listed in the area heading, together with their two-letter abbreviations that appear after grid references in the text.

Each area is briefly described in geographical and historical terms before details are given of the archaeological sites. Information of more general interest is kept to a minimum, since this is easily available in publications which are revised annually (see p. 28). In particular no attempt has been made to recommend individual hotels and eating-places. The touring bases suggested usually offer some choice of price and quality, but the standard reference books will reveal many wayside alternatives, especially for those who want to combine gastronomy with their archaeology, or who prefer country solitude to the convenience of a market town.

Selection and Grading of Sites

The archaeological sites mentioned amount to a very small proportion of the total available to anyone who wants to study a particular area, period or type of structure in detail. The published works used in the selection of sites are of varying reliability and completeness, as determined by the personal interest and territory of former fieldworkers, the evolving standards of recording, and not least the progress of county surveys. For example, the Royal Commission's Caernarvonshire volumes describe some 1,200 pre-Norman sites, of which only 86 are mentioned here. Cardiganshire, by contrast, has not been comprehensively surveyed, and reliable information can be obtained only from separate studies of stone circles, hillforts, the Roman period, and so on, with the result that the selection of 42 sites in that county may be poorly balanced in an overall view of Wales.

In choosing sites from the basic sources, and in grading them as *primary* or *secondary*, priority has generally been given to the most accessible and best preserved. Archaeological importance, however, has properly been allowed to override those two qualities to a considerable extent, either when the site is a prime example of its type, or on grounds of individuality. Finally, the hard-earned evidence of excavation has been taken into account, along with accidental discoveries, in the inclusion of some *additional* sites which do not justify a visit (if indeed they have not been destroyed), but which form part of the emerging picture of Welsh archaeology.

Primary Sites
INV   *123 456* AN
which form the basis of the tours, are named thus in bold type as paragraph headings. **Secondary sites,** for extension of the tours, are also in bold type, but are contained in continuous narrative. *Additional sites*, not recommended for visits, are named in italics.

References to literature are generally given only for primary sites and are limited to accessible works from which some useful detail may be obtained, as well as a lead to other works. The abbreviations used, appearing in italic type below the site names, simplify the identification of the full titles in the Bibliography (p. 194).

National Grid References are given in italics for all sites, and consist only of the six figures which identify their position in the 100 km square concerned. For an explanation of the National Grid see p. 26. The two-letter abbreviations after the figures refer to the counties listed in area headings.

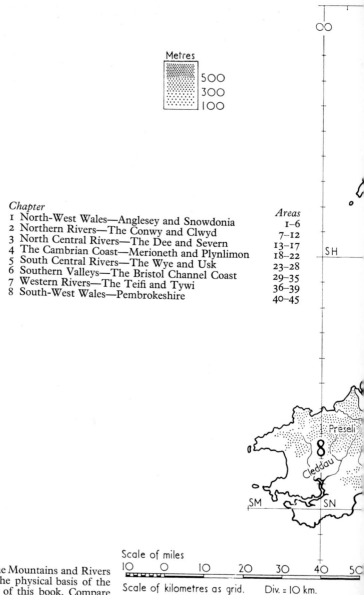

Metres
500
300
100

S H

Preseli

8

Cleddau

SM   SN

Scale of miles
10   0   10   20   30   40   50

Scale of kilometres as grid.   Div. = 10 km.

SR   SS

Figure 1. The Mountains and Rivers of Wales: The physical basis of the subdivisions of this book. Compare Fig. 2.

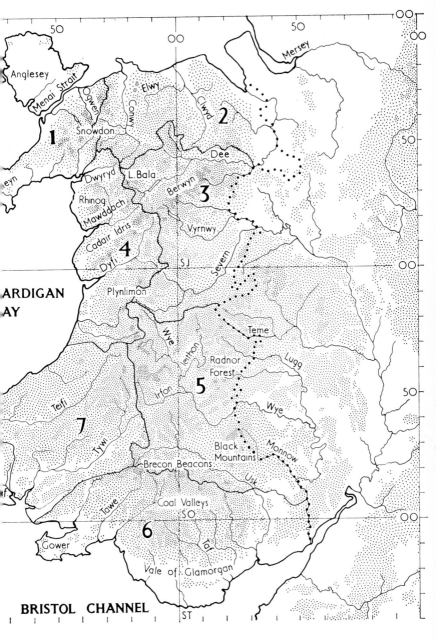

Anglesey

Menai Strait

Ogwen

Elwy

Conwy

Clwyd

Mersey

1

Snowdon

2

Lleyn

Dwyryd

L. Bala

Dee

Rhinog

Berwyn

3

Mawddach

Cadair Idris

Vyrnwy

4

Dyfi

SJ

Severn

CARDIGAN

BAY

Plynlimon

Teme

Wye

Radnor
Forest

Lugg

Ithon

Irfon

5

Wye

Teifi

7

Tywi

Black
Mountains

Monnow

Brecon Beacons

Usk

Tawe

Coal Valleys

SO

6

Gower

Taf

Vale of Glamorgan

BRISTOL CHANNEL

ST

Area		Suggested centre
1	Anglesey North-West	Holyhead
2	Anglesey South-East	Bangor
3	The Lleyn Peninsula	Pwllheli
4	Snowdon South	Portmadoc
5	Snowdon North	Caernarvon
6	The Ogwen	Bangor
7	The Lower Conwy	Llandudno
8	The Upper Conwy	Betws-y-coed
9	The Elwy	Colwyn Bay
10	The Upper Clwyd	Ruthin
11	The Lower Clwyd	Rhyl
12	The Lower Dee	Wrexham
13	The Middle Dee	Llangollen
14	The Upper Dee	Bala
15	The Vyrnwy	Llanfyllin
16	The Middle Severn	Welshpool
17	The Upper Severn	Newtown
18	The Dwyryd	Harlech
19	The Rhinogs West	Barmouth
20	The Mawddach	Dolgellau
21	The Dyfi	Machynlleth
22	Plynlimon West	Aberystwyth
23	The Upper Wye	Rhayader
24	The Irfon and Ieithon	Llandrindod Wells
25	Radnor Forest	Knighton
26	The Middle Wye	Hay-on-Wye
27	The Upper Usk	Brecon
28	The Middle Usk and Monnow	Abergavenny
29	The Lower Wye	Chepstow
30	The Lower Usk	Newport, Mon.
31	Vale of Glamorgan East	Cardiff
32	Vale of Glamorgan West	Bridgend
33	The Eastern Coal Valleys	Aberdare
34	The Western Coal Valleys	Neath
35	The Gower Peninsula	Swansea
36	The Upper Tywi	Llandovery
37	The Lower Tywi	Carmarthen
38	The Upper Teifi	Lampeter
39	The Lower Teifi	Newcastle Emlyn
40	The Carmarthenshire Taf	Laugharne
41	Preseli North	Newport, Pemb.
42	The Cleddau	Haverfordwest
43	The St. Davids Peninsula	St. Davids
44	The Milford Peninsula	Haverfordwest
45	The Tenby Peninsula	Tenby

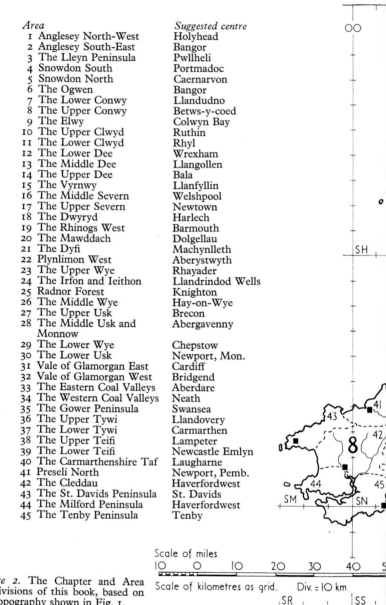

Scale of miles

10   0   10   20   30   40   5

Scale of kilometres as grid.   Div. = 10 km.

Figure 2. The Chapter and Area subdivisions of this book, based on the topography shown in Fig. 1.

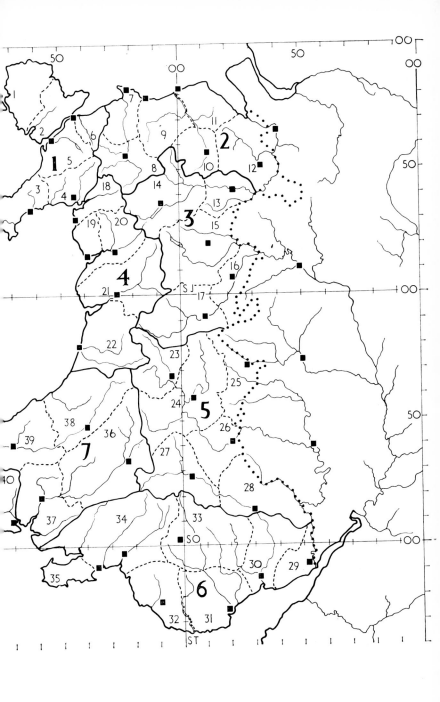

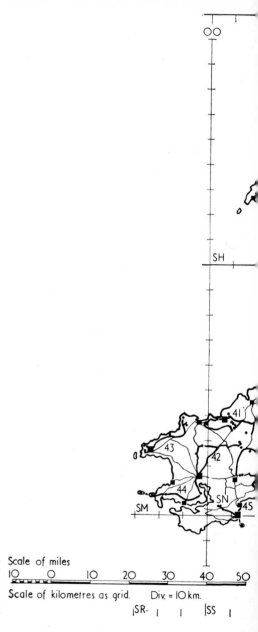

Figure 3. The main roads of Wales, with minor roads added to complete the recommended tours from towns shown on Fig. 2. Small squares indicate alternative centres, and dots represent main archaeological sites.

Scale of miles

10   0   10   20   30   40   50

Scale of kilometres as grid.   Div. = 10 km.

SR   SS

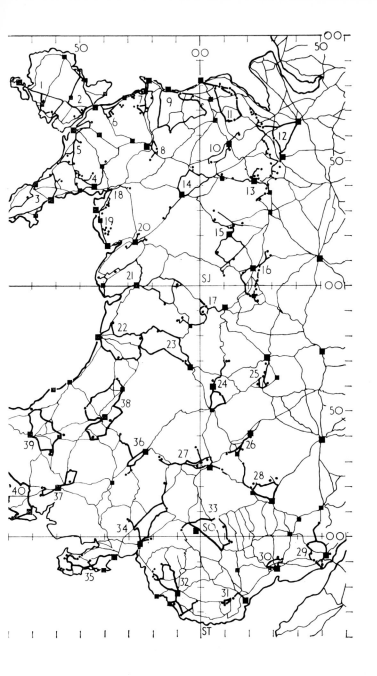

ORDNANCE SURVEY MAPS
AND THE NATIONAL GRID

Though there are other excellent maps, some of which may give a better idea of topography, Ordnance Survey maps are recommended since they are based on a logical progression of scales related to the metric system and the National Grid. *For tour planning* the special 'quarter-inch' (1 : 250,000) map of Wales should be used in conjunction with Figs. 1–3. Most minor roads are shown, and villages named, while hill-shading gives a good idea of the lie of the land. *For location of sites* use the 'one-inch' or the 1 : 50,000 series, both of which show most antiquities and established rights of way. Grid references in this book relate to these series, of which map numbers are given in area headings. *For greater detail*, including field boundaries which may help in negotiating the countryside, the '2½-inch' series (1 : 25,000) may be used, but is by no means essential. *For research purposes* on limited areas the large-scale '6-inch' maps (1 : 10,560, now being replaced by a new series at 1 : 10,000) and '25-inch' plans (1 : 2,500) are invaluable, but are not recommended for touring purposes. *Archaeological period maps*, with gazetteers of all known sites, include *Ancient Britain* (1964) and *Southern Britain in the Iron Age* (1962) at 10 miles/inch, and *Roman Britain* (1956) and *Britain in the Dark Ages* (1966) at 16 miles/inch.

The National Grid is a reference system used on all current Ordnance Survey maps to give a unique definition for any point in Britain. The sides of grid squares represent decimal multiples in the metric system, numbered at map edges; decimal subdivisions can be estimated within the squares to give greater precision. Thus on the one-inch/1 : 50,000 series a six-figure reference, given in this book in two groups of three, can be simply applied as follows:

The first two figures of the first group can be found at the top or bottom edge of the map, where values increase eastwards; the third figure represents tenths estimated eastwards. The second group is then used at the sides of the map, where values increase northwards. The site can be found at the intersection of these co-ordinates. It can be seen that on a larger-scale map it is possible to estimate a fourth figure for each group, making an eight-figure reference. References derived in this way are unique only within a square of 100 km side, but cannot repeat on a single one-inch map. If necessary to avoid confusion with another 100 km square, two distinguishing letters can be added before the figures. These are shown on the Maps (Figs. 1–3); they are also used in the numbering of $2\frac{1}{2}$-inch maps.

Place Names. The spelling of Welsh place names follows the recommendations of the Board of Celtic Studies of the University of Wales where this is feasible without introducing doubt. An anglicised version of a name will still be used if it is in common use, or if it has been accepted for use on Ordnance Survey maps.

GENERAL INFORMATION

The Wales Tourist Board (Bwrdd Croeso i Cymru), Welcome House, High St., Llandaff, Cardiff CF5 2YZ, *does not deal with bookings*, but can supply the addresses of information offices in most holiday towns and localities, either under local authorities or at special centres for bodies such as National Parks. The Board publishes annually three *Holiday Guides* (for *South and West, Mid,* and *North Wales*), which give historical and touring information as well as selected accommodation and notes on outdoor pursuits. The latter are treated at greater length in separate pamphlets.

The British Tourist Authority, 64 St. James's St., London SW1A 1NF, *does not deal with bookings*, but co-ordinates information on holiday services for the whole of Britain through national and regional bodies. It has information available on subjects of interest to the holiday-maker, as well as accommodation lists, including camping sites. The B.T.A. has offices in the U.S.A. at 680 Fifth Avenue, N.Y. 10019; 612 South Flower St., Los Angeles, Calif. 90017; John Hancock Center (Suite 2450), 875 North Michigan Ave., Chicago, Ill. 60611; also in many other countries.

Information on hotels and restaurants is best sought in the many guides available in bookshops, as well as through the motoring organisations.

State Archaeology
Official publications on archaeology (listed by H.M. Stationery Office in their free *Sectional List No. 27*, which is periodically revised) are obtainable from Government Bookshops—for *Wales* at 109 St. Mary St., Cardiff CF1 1JW; *also* at 80 Chichester St., Belfast BT1 4JY; 258 Broad St., Birmingham B1 2HE; 50 Fairfax St., Bristol BS1 3DE; 13a Castle St., Edinburgh EH2 3AR; 49 High Holborn, London W.C.1 (callers); P.O. Box 569, London S.E.1 (mail); Brazennose St., Manchester M60 8AS; in *U.S.A.* at British Information Services, 845 Third Avenue, N.Y. 10022. There are agents for H.M.S.O. in most Commonwealth and foreign countries. Ordnance Survey maps are available from the International Map Company, 140 Liberty St., New York, N.Y. 10006. In addition, any bookseller can obtain the items listed, and may have site guides of local interest in stock (see Bibliography, p. 194).

The Royal Commission on Ancient Monuments in Wales and Monmouth-shire (including the National Monuments Record for Wales), Edleston House, Queens Rd., Aberystwyth, is concerned solely with survey and recording, as published in its county *Inventories.*

The Inspectorate of Ancient Monuments (of the Department of the Environment), Central Office for Wales, Gabalfa, Cardiff, is responsible to the Welsh Office for the protection of all field monuments. It publishes a list of over 1,200, whose preservation is considered to be of national importance, in addition to maintaining 32 prehistoric and Roman sites. Either of the above-named bodies will be grateful to receive information concerning unwarranted disturbance of known sites, or the discovery of new ones. Chance finds of objects, however, are more properly the concern of the National Museum of Wales, or the nearest local museum.

National Museums and Societies
There is much to be gained from contact with museums (and public libraries) which are often the centre of local archaeological activity. *The National Museum of Wales,* Cathays Park, Cardiff, advises and serves its affiliated museums throughout Wales. (Relevant ones are listed below.) *The Council for British Archaeology,* through its Group 2 for Wales, which publishes an annual bulletin *Archaeology in Wales* (Hon. Secretary, Miss Frances Lynch, University College of North Wales, Bangor), provides a forum for contact between archaeological societies. *The Cambrian Archaeological Association,* founded 1846, publishes material of national importance in *Archaeologia Cambrensis,* arranges annual conferences, and sponsors excavations and research projects.

County and District Societies (many small but active groups not listed)
Anglesey Antiquarian Soc. *Brecknock* Soc. *Caernarvonshire* Historical Soc. *Cardiganshire* Antiquarian Soc. *Carmarthenshire* Antiquarian Soc. & Field Club. *Denbighshire* Historical Soc. *Flintshire* Historical Soc. *Glamorgan:* Cardiff Naturalists Soc.; Gower Soc. *Merioneth* Historical and Record Soc. *Monmouthshire* and Caerleon Antiquarian Assoc. *Montgomeryshire:* The Powysland Club. The *Radnorshire* Soc.

Local Museums (mentioned in text under Area numbers given)
Brecknock: County Mus., Brecon (27). *Caernarvonshire:* Mus. of Welsh

Antiquities, Bangor (2, 6); Rapallo House Mus., Llandudno (7); Segontium Mus., Caernarvon (5). *Cardiganshire*: Ceredigion Mus., Aberystwyth (22). *Carmarthenshire*: County Mus., Carmarthen (37). *Denbighshire*: Plas Newydd Mus., Llangollen (13). *Flintshire*: St. Asaph Cathedral Mus. (11). *Glamorgan*: Royal Institution of South Wales, Swansea (35). *Monmouthshire*: Abergavenny & District Mus. (28); Legionary Mus., Caerleon (30); Newport Mus. (28). *Montgomeryshire*: Powysland Mus., Welshpool (16). *Pembrokeshire*: County Mus., Haverfordwest (42, 44); Tenby Mus. (45). *Radnorshire*: County Mus., Llandrindod Wells (24).

AN OUTLINE OF THE ARCHAEOLOGY OF WALES

The division of Wales into manageable areas follows topographical features in preference to modern boundaries, to preserve greater relevance to the prehistoric periods with which the book is largely concerned. Mountain ridges have been chosen for boundaries rather than rivers, to assist the planning of tours based on valley routes, but this should not be allowed to disguise the fact that some prehistoric people, notably in the Bronze Age, are more likely to have regarded rivers as territorial limits. For the mixed farming economy of the neolithic and iron-age populations it was river valleys and lower mountain slopes that invited movement and deeper penetration, giving a detectable uniformity of structural type to the field monuments of the greater valleys (the basis used for Chapters 3, 5–7). A different cause has determined the uniformity of those regions where mountain masses abut on the sea, leaving only narrow areas of coastal plain with less dissection by rivers (Chapters 1, 2, 4, 8). Here the most direct access was from the sea, and it is no surprise to find that the closest cultural links extend to north and south for some distance along the western seaways, or even to the other side of the Irish Sea.

Because of the topographical arrangement of the sites to be visited, this outline is needed to provide an immediate frame of reference for use in the field. It is not intended to be a substitute for background reading (see Bibliography, p. 194). By the distinction of certain terms in **bold face** it will also serve as a glossary of the special meanings in which archaeology abounds, while sites named will provide good examples of their kind (A in parenthesis indicates Area).

A few terms of a general nature need separate definition: *Cropmarks and soilmarks* on air photographs indicate the presence of buried features not visible at ground level, which affect growing crops or soil humidity.

Culture. From many shades of meaning only one need apply here—the total assemblage of material manifestations that indicates affinity between otherwise independent population units.

Industry. A distinctive range of tool types (especially flint) that may characterise a site and form the basis of culture assessment.

Radiocarbon dating is a technique of physics that enables the probable

date of an organic relic to be assessed, relying on the known rate of
decay of the carbon 14 isotope.

The Stone Age

The **Palaeolithic** or Old Stone Age covers the whole of human existence down to about 9000 B.C., when the last of the ice sheets had
retreated from the mainland of Europe, having covered the whole of
Wales apart from a narrow strip on the south coast. The **caves** of
Areas 9, 11, 35, 40, 45, to which man had retreated for safety or warmth
at various times, are the sole source of information about this remote
period, and it is only at the end of the **Upper Palaeolithic** that flint
tools can be compared with the main trend of European development, in
the **Upper** and **Final** stages of the **Aurignacian** culture (type site,
Aurignac, S.W. France). The skeleton from Paviland (A 35) establishes
a link at about 16,500 B.C. with the physical type named at the French
site of **Crô-Magnon,** and the last cave-dwellers (Cat Hole, A 35)
belonged to the **Creswellian** tradition developed independently in
Britain. The only example of cave art claimed for Wales is not now
considered acceptable (Bacon Hole, A 35).

With the gradual post-glacial improvement of climate in the **Mesolithic** or Middle Stone Age, down to about 4000 B.C., the mountains and
coasts of Wales were reoccupied by people whose most distinctive relics
are the small flint **microliths** used as the points and barbs of their
specialised hunting and fishing equipment. The only surface trace of
their insubstantial settlements is an occasional scatter of waste flint,
though some caves and rock-shelters (Caldey Island, A 45) contain tool
types directly developed from the Upper Palaeolithic.

In the **Neolithic** Period (from about 5000 B.C.) there began to arrive
in Britain small bands of people in search of new land for the agricultural way of life that had spread slowly across Europe from the
Near East. Settlements with timber houses are occassionally found, but
only by chance and not from surface traces (Clegyr Boia, A 43; Sant-y-
nyll, A 31). Domestic equipment included **leaf-shaped flint arrowheads** and **polished stone axes**; **pottery** appeared for the first time,
hand-made and round-bottomed, of plain 'western' type in the
earliest tombs and settlements, but heavily moulded and decorated on
later sites, variously named after type sites such as **Peterborough**.

The most common neolithic structures are the **megalithic** tombs,
consisting of chambers and passages of large upright stones combined
with dry walling, roofed with massive **capstones** or with smaller slabs

overlapping inwards as **corbelling**. The large covering mounds have often been entirely robbed or eroded, to leave the main chambers standing alone as **cromlechs** (traditionally associated, but quite falsely, with the activities of Druids). These were the communal vaults of local communities, and show a variety of constructional types derived by stages from different parts of the continental mainland over a span of some 3,000 years. In common with much of western Europe, the **long cairn** of stone or **long barrow** of earth was the earliest form, with three main varieties of internal layout: the **portal dolmen** of the Irish Sea area (Dyffryn, A 19; Carreg Coetan Arthur, Pentre Ifan, A 41); the **segmented gallery** of north Irish and south Scottish character (Trefignath, A 1); and the **transepted gallery** of the Severn-Cotswold group (Capel Garmon, A 8; Tŷ-isaf, A 28; Parc Cwm, A 35). Somewhat later were the **passage graves** (Barclodiad y Gawres, A 1; Bryn Celli Ddu, A 2), built in round mounds and displaying the **megalithic art** tradition that they shared with the fine tombs of the Irish Boyne region.

In the middle of neolithic times appeared a different burial tradition by **cremation** in **henge monuments** (Llandegai, A 6), so named from the occasional use of upright settings of stones or timber. Now also began the trading of stone axes in **roughout** form from **axe factories** at sources of suitable igneous rock (Mynydd Rhiw, A 3; Graig Lwyd, A 7), matching the output of flint mines elsewhere. By about 2000 B.C. neolithic cultural distinctions had become blurred by contact and fusion into an overall pattern in which megalithic tombs were either poor derivatives of earlier types or had even given way to the use of caves as ready-made substitutes (Areas 11, 12). Subsistence was probably a fair mixture of crop and animal husbandry, though hunting and fishing were no doubt still of considerable importance.

The last neolithic immigrants from the continent are characterised by the drinking vessels that have determined our name for them. At first **Beaker** people buried their dead singly in a crouched posture in slab-lined **cists** or in pits under round mounds (Brymbo, A 12), but a considerable degree of integration is indicated by their use of existing megalithic tombs (Tinkinswood, A 31). They seem also to have played an active part in religious developments involving henge monuments and **stone circles,** for it was they who came to Pembrokeshire for the Stonehenge bluestones (Area 41) and used the later of the Llandegai circles about 1850 B.C. Some of the smaller stone circles and **alignments** of the mountains (Areas 15, 21, 27, 34, 40, 42) are almost certainly their work, or follow their ideas in the ensuing Early Bronze Age.

C

The Bronze Age

The Beaker people had copper for daggers and pins, but it was not long before the neolithic population in general adopted bronze technology and trade, searching out tin for their alloy and gold for their finest craft work (Area 12). The greatest concentration of wealth lay beyond the Severn, but a direct link with Wessex can be detected in the presence of **bell-barrows** (Cors y Carneddau, A 7; Crug yr Afan, A 33), so named from their profile, in which the mound is separated from the ditch by a narrow shelf **(berm)** at original ground level.

Cremation now became established as the sole burial rite, either beneath a **round barrow** or **cairn**, or at least contained in a slab-lined cist or pit within a **ring cairn** or a **stone-kerbed platform**. Many sites display elaborate stages of construction when excavated, and frequent re-use for **secondary burials** later in the period (Areas 12, 14, 18, 19, 22, 27, 32, 34). Most burials were accompanied by distinctive **grave goods**, notably the special funerary pottery **(cinerary urns** and **incense cups)** developed from flat-based types of **food vessel**.

Other characteristic monuments of the Bronze Age include the arrays of **cupmarks**, of assumed ritual purpose, on suitable rock slabs, including parts of chambered tombs already recognised as sacred sites (Bachwen, A 5; Maen Cattwg, A 33; Trelyffant, A 41). **Standing stones** (Welsh **'maen hir'**, *pl.* **'meini hirion'**) were in many cases isolated burial markers, but were also associated with cairns or circles (Areas 1, 5, 7, 21, 23, 27, 32, 34, 37, 41–45), or were used as trackway markers (Areas 18, 20).

Settlements of the earlier Bronze Age are hardly known, and for the end of the period it can only be supposed that some mountain pastoral sites and hilltops were occupied before the beginning of the Iron Age. One certain indication of domestic activity, however, is the occurrence of open-air **hearths** near streams, surrounded by heaps of burnt stone used for the trough-cooking of hunted game (Cefn Trefor-isaf, A 4).

The Iron Age

In about the VII century B.C. there began a succession of immigrations of Celtic people who reimposed on the countryside a definite pattern of agricultural settlement. No precise date can be given to the start of the **Iron Age**, for although the new metal was known, it was rare at first, and bronze continued in common use (Llyn Fawr, A 33). For Britain as a whole the traditional sequence of **Iron Age A**, **B** and **C** can now be elaborated by the recognition of regional cultures and stages in their development, but in general terms it is enough to think of **Iron Age A** as the primary Celtic settlement, absorbing or subduing the bronze-age population; **Iron Age B** is seen in the arrival of fresh immigrants over-flowing from continental **La Tène** cultures, reaching Wales and the southern Marches in coastwise and overland movements from the III century B.C.; **Iron Age C** movements are virtually historical, being the direct result of the pressure of the Roman Empire on the minor king-doms of Gaul and southern Britain before the Roman conquest of Wales.

For Wales the Iron Age sequence has been well demonstrated by excavation in **hillforts** of the south-east (Llanmelin, Sudbrook, A 29), strongholds built by communal effort, with progressive refinements of construction and elaboration of the plan; other major forts no doubt served as focal points of tribal power in other regions (Dinorben, A 9; Ffridd Faldwyn, A 16; Pen Dinas, A 22; etc.). Extra protection might be provided for the entrance approach by outworks such as the **barbican** (Burfa Camp, A 25; Llanmelin, A 29) or **chevaux-de-frise** (Pen y Gaer, A 7), and the gateways themselves might be improved from simple gaps by lengthening the rampart ends inwards. The defensive circuit was usually improved by turning an original **univallate** (single-ramparted) fort into a **bivallate** or **multivallate** one, in which the greater depth of defence was well suited to the use of the sling.

Much of the variety in hillforts is due to choice of site and the nature of building material. Most common is the contour fort, where the principal **rampart** follows a natural brow, but the inclusion of crags and cliffs made the task easier (Craig yr Aderyn, A 21; Craig Rhiwarth, A 15; The Breiddin, A 16). For coastal dwellers the ideal was a sea-girt **promontory fort** (Areas 1, 21, 32, 35, 43–45), where a narrow neck of level ground would be the only part of the circuit needing defence. On scree-covered slopes the whole rampart can be a massive stone wall (Caer y Twr, A 1; Garn Fadrun etc., A 3), with faces slightly sloped **(battered)** for stability, and topped by a **breastwork** protecting a **wall-walk.** Alternatively the inner and outer faces might consist of slabs and boulders set up as **orthostats** to contain a rubble filling (Conway Mountain, A 7). A ditch was usually dug outside a rampart only when the ground lacked natural steepness, or to provide extra material. Where surface stone was not to hand, the whole front **scarp** of the rampart might consist of a slope continuing to the bottom of a deep, rock-cut ditch, often faced with stone quarried uphill or brought from nearby beaches; on the outer lip of the ditch a smaller, **counterscarp** bank might be an added obstacle.

Most defended sites have less than one hectare (2.47 acres) of enclosed area, and are likely to have served as simple refuges rather than as permanently manned forts. Some of the very smallest, however, must be **fortified homesteads** of people farming the surrounding land (Moel Fodig, A 14; Carn Alw, A 41; Hardings Down West, A 35). The evidence for domestic structures is uneven, since perishable building material alone may have been used in some regions. In the west and north-west, **hut-circles** had low stone walls on which the rafters rested, and lay dispersed among the enclosures of **pastoral settlements** (Braich y Gornel, A 4; Moel Faban, A 6), or were securely grouped in their own enclosures where domestic and industrial activities took place (Hafoty Wern-las, A 5). These **enclosed hut-groups** constitute evidence of the continuity of the native population through the Roman occupation, with a tendency to straight walling, but only excavation can give a site a certain pre- or post-Roman date (Din Lligwy, A 2; Caerau, A 5). The same areas of early fields continued in use, the so-called 'celtic fields' of roughly rectangular shape, lined with walling of stones cleared from the ground, which developed into **lynchets** on slopes through the accumulation of soil behind them and erosion in front (Areas 3–7, 18–20).

The Roman Period

The **Roman occupation** of Wales was at first a military affair, undertaken in two decisive campaigns in A.D. 74 and 78, as the second stage of the conquest of southern Britain. Some of the temporary **marching camps** of legionary troops on the move (Y Pigwn, A 27; Blaen-cwmbach, A 34) must belong to these campaigns, and to earlier ones which had met fierce resistance from the Silures of south-east Wales. The territory was divided between two main legionary commands, Deva (Chester) in the north, and Isca (Caerleon, A 30) in the south.

A complete network of **auxiliary forts**, connected by well-engineered **roads**, was soon established (examples in most Areas), but several do not seem to have been fully manned for long. Others in key positions were transformed into permanent bases by the addition of stone to the initial earth-and-timber structures (Tomen y Mur, A 18; Segontium, A 5; Castell Collen, A 24; Gelligaer, A 33; Neath, A 34). Troops on exercise while stationed there built small **practice camps** during instruction in field defence techniques, and they also presumably manned the **signal stations** on the connecting roads (Hirfynydd, A 34). Several **milestones** have survived (museums at Segontium, A 5; Swansea, A 34; etc.), but only a few stretches of actual road display a good built-up **agger** of metalling unaltered by modern use (Areas 7, 24, 27, 34, 38).

The Roman imperial objective was normally to follow initial occupation, whether achieved by force or treaty, with civil administration. Caerwent (A 29) was soon established as a tribal capital for the Silures, and Carmarthen (A 37) for the Demetae. **Villas** built by favoured landowners in the southern countryside (Llantwit Major, A 32; Ely, A 31) helped to preserve the social order and commercial life. In remoter areas commerce was promoted through the growth of civil settlements around the forts, and through the exploitation of minerals. Dolaucothi (A 36) is beginning to reveal a complex history of both civil and military presence at the gold mines, similar to the control exercised over copper and lead mining (Parys Mountain, A 2; Ffrith, A 12).

Outside southern Wales the Roman colonial pattern does not seem to have sucessfully replaced native forms of settlement, though Roman influence was strong (Hafoty Wern-las, A 5; Cwmbrwyn, A 40). Native sites have yielded fine red **Samian** pottery, alongside coins and plenty of coarse pottery. It even seems to have been part of colonial policy to allow occupation of some of the larger hillforts (Tre'r Ceiri, A 3; Dinorben, A 9; The Breiddin, A 16), though without fortification.

The Post-Roman Period

The increasingly nervous state of Roman imperial control through the III and IV centuries is marked by military and civilian defensive works. The late forts at Caer Gybi (A 1) and Cardiff (A 31) were built against the threat of roving pirates, and the walls of Caerwent (A 29) were strengthened. After the official Roman withdrawal of A.D. 410 the natives were left to their own defence. Little is known of the history of this Dark Age, apart from the identification of some well-protected settlements (Pant-y-saer, A 2; Dinas Emrys, A 4; Dinas Powis, A 31), and the meagre evidence of **inscribed stones**, in both Latin and Irish **(ogam)** characters. The survival of a Roman pattern of administration is suggested (Penmachno, A 8; Carmarthen, A 37) along with the firmly established Christian religion.

On the east also the Celt had to face the Anglo-Saxons of Mercia and Wessex. Rulers and events are dimly recorded in heroic literature, but hardly at all on monuments (Catamanus, A 1; Eliseg's Pillar, A 13). The great **dykes** of Wat and Offa (Areas 11–13, 16, 25, 26) are the finest memorials to the success of the Welsh princes in staving off the threat of submergence, and establishing by treaty their right to independence.

METRIC CONVERSION TABLES

AREA 1 hectare = 2.5 acres approx. 1 acre = 0.4 ha approx.

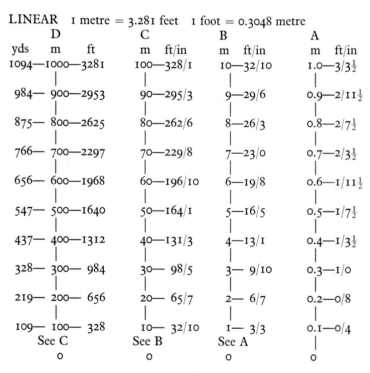

hectares given above acre equivalents at left, acres only to same scale at right.

LINEAR 1 metre = 3.281 feet 1 foot = 0.3048 metre

D			C		B		A	
yds	m	ft	m	ft/in	m	ft/in	m	ft/in
1094—	1000—	3281	100—	328/1	10—	32/10	1.0—	3/3½
984—	900—	2953	90—	295/3	9—	29/6	0.9—	2/11½
875—	800—	2625	80—	262/6	8—	26/3	0.8—	2/7½
766—	700—	2297	70—	229/8	7—	23/0	0.7—	2/3½
656—	600—	1968	60—	196/10	6—	19/8	0.6—	1/11½
547—	500—	1640	50—	164/1	5—	16/5	0.5—	1/7½
437—	400—	1312	40—	131/3	4—	13/1	0.4—	1/3½
328—	300—	984	30—	98/5	3—	9/10	0.3—	1/0
219—	200—	656	20—	65/7	2—	6/7	0.2—	0/8
109—	100—	328	10—	32/10	1—	3/3	0.1—	0/4
	See C		See B		See A			
	o		o		o		o	

1 NORTH-WEST WALES
Anglesey and Snowdonia

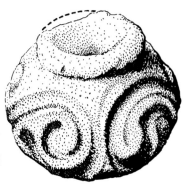

Figure 4. The upper stone of a rotary quern from a II century A.D. hut group in Anglesey, with traditional Celtic curvilinear design. Scale 1:10. *National Museum of Wales.*

ANGLESEY NORTH-WEST   58 km (36 miles)
AREA I   Anglesey AN
Map 114; 1″ 106; 2½″ SH *27, 28, 36–39*

So many thousands of people use Holyhead only as a staging post between Ireland and the British mainland, that it is pleasant to emphasise its other role as a holiday base for the whole of western Anglesey. The popularity of the sandy beaches has also led to the growth of small centres like Rhosneigr, where lodging is easily found. Historically this is an island of scattered village settlements, many of which have retained their agricultural peace.

Topographically Anglesey as a whole presents a worn-down appearance, with many low-lying marshy areas between ridges of the most ancient rocks. The north-western part of the island was particularly unfavourable for prehistoric settlement, the only Iron Age concentration being around Holyhead Mountain. The variety of the megalithic tomb architecture, though implying at least a constant neolithic population, is perhaps more a reflection of the island's position in the western sea route.

The more elusive Bronze Age population has left its mark in the standing stones which are presumed to mark their burials. Convenient examples of these *meini hirion* ('long stones') are at **Llanfaethlu** (*319 863*) and **Penyrorsedd** (*333 093 & 333 906*), ranging from 2.6 m to 3.7 m in height. In a different Bronze Age tradition are the round cairns which have produced multiple cremation burials, such as *Bedd Branwen* (*361 849*), recently re-excavated after 150 years. Here were at

39

least a dozen cremations, with cinerary urns, jet and amber beads and a
bone knife pommel as grave goods.

Somewhat remote on the north and south coasts respectively are two
Iron Age promontory forts with contrasting defensive schemes:
Dinas Gynfor (*391 951*) has two ramparts crossing a wide neck of land,
the entrance way being in a natural gully, while at **Twyn-y-parc**
(*368 650*) the land connection is narrow and is protected by a single
massive rampart with two smaller banks outside, and a short stretch of
terracing on the N.W. to strengthen a weak part of the natural cliff.

The Catamanus Stone
INV p. 87   *383 693* AN
A memorial stone of the post-Roman era is housed in Llangadwaladr
Church, bearing a Latin inscription to Cadfan (died *c.* 625; grandfather
of the patron saint Cadwaladr), describing him as 'the wisest and most
illustrious of rulers'. Precise historical ascriptions of this kind are all
too rarely possible.

Barclodiad y Gawres
Pl. 2; *PA* p. 34 and *BG*   *328 708* AN
'The apronful of the giantess' is a round cairn containing one of the
most exciting neolithic discoveries of post-war years, a series of five
decorated stones in the passage and chambers of a classic cruciform
passage grave. The variety of spirals, lozenges, zigzags and chevrons,
laboriously pecked out on their surfaces, link the tomb stylistically with
those of the Irish Boyne culture, with a common origin in Iberia. No
capstones remain, but a dome has been built for protection. In State
care, access by prior arrangement at 22 The Square, Caernarvon,
pending better alternative; a pamphlet is available.

Tynewydd Burial Chamber
PA p. 28   *344 738* AN
The coverstone on three original uprights is remarkable for its size, but
there is little else to give cultural definition. The only datable finds from
excavation indicate re-use of the chamber in the Bronze Age. In State
care, open always without charge.

Trefignath Burial Chamber
PA p. 30   *258 805* AN
A long, segmented megalithic tomb, with portal stones over 2 m high
at the E. end. The first compartment is more complete than the others

Plate 2. Barclodiad y Gawres (Area 1): one of the upright stones decorated with 'megalithic art' motifs. Scale in feet. *Photo: M. J. O'Kelly.*

Plate 3. Llyn Cerrig Bach hoard (Area 1): reconstruction of a pre-Roman chariot. *Photo: National Museum of Wales.*

(there were once at least three), and the covering mound has gone, but enough remains to suggest a link with the megalithic tradition of the northern Irish Sea province. In State care, open always without charge.

A short distance N.W. of Trefignath is a good standing stone at **Ty-mawr** (*254 810*), and at **Penrhos-Feilw** (*227 809*) is a pair 3.4 m apart. All three are in State care, accessible at any time without charge.

On and near Holy Island many aspects of the Iron Age are represented, spanning both the pre-Roman and Roman phases. The deposit of 138 bronze, iron and wooden objects of 'the last 200 years or so of Celtic independence' found at *Llyn Cerrig Bach* (*305 766*; *LCB*) is in the National Museum of Wales. Here is a mine of evidence on the British development of the La Tène artistic tradition, in local terms indicating the importance of Anglesey as a focus of wealth, probably in the hands of a priestly caste. (Plate 3.)

The small promontory fort of **Dinas** (*223 794*), almost cut off by the sea and defended on the landward cliff by only a slight bank, is possibly pre-Roman; but finds from the open settlement at **Porth Dafarch** (*235 802*) showed occupation covering the III to V centuries A.D. The best hillfort and open settlement, however, are on Holyhead Mountain itself.

Caer y Twr
PA p. 227   *219 831* AN
About 7 ha at the summit of the mountain are enclosed by the addition

of a strong stone rampart to the natural crags. The best stretch is at the
N. and E. where it stands 3 m high in places, and visible detail includes
a rampart walk and a breastwork 2 m thick. There are no huts inside,
and the rampart at the N.W. seems to have been deliberately destroyed,
perhaps as a considered act of Roman colonial policy. In State care,
open always without charge.

Ty-mawr Hut Group
INV p. 24   *212 820* AN

On a natural terrace about twenty huts remain of the fifty originally
recorded in an area of 6–8 ha. Lying in two groups, they comprise
circular dwellings up to 10 m in diameter, and attached subrectangular
chambers, typically 4 m long by 1.5 m. The low walls are mostly built of
laid stone, but some have upright facing slabs. Excavation finds included
domestic querns, mortars and spindlewhorls, but copper slag, coins and
III/IV century coarse pottery give closer definition to this native
settlement during the Roman occupation. The suggestion in the name
Cytiau Gwyddelod that these were the huts of Irishmen (Goidels), driven
out by Brythonic Celts in the V century according to tradition, is not
supported by the finds. In State care, open always without charge.

Caer Gybi
RFW p. 135   *246 827* AN

The stone wall with solid corner towers round St. Cybi's Church,
enclosing an area 75 m long by 48 m, is probably a 'shore fort' built *c.*
A.D. 300 to protect the decaying Roman empire from barbarian raiders.
It is well preserved to the level of the rampart walk 6 m above the original
ground level. In State care, open always without charge.

ANGLESEY SOUTH-EAST   64 km (40 miles)
AREA 2   Anglesey AN
Map 114; 1" 106; 2½" SH *46–49, 56–58, 67, 68*

In the east of Anglesey there are again all the holiday amenities, and
accommodation to suit all tastes, notably at Benllech, at the former
copper-mining centre of Amlwch, and in the historic town of Beaumaris,
where Edward I's castle of 1295 deserves a special visit. Llangefni

would serve well as a tourist centre, and the university town of Bangor is as convenient for this area as it is for the mainland (for Bangor Museum see Area 6).

South-eastern Anglesey, though basically similar to the north-west, has a greater proportion of well-drained ground and is richer in sites of all periods. The present-day road and rail links afforded by the two fine XVIII century bridges (built by Telford and Stephenson respectively) have lessened the reality of the strait as an isolating barrier. In a different role it also offered a more hospitable passage for the earliest sea venturers than the circuit of the island, resulting in a greater variety of megalithic tomb types and other evidence of neolithic settlement. For the Celtic Iron Age population the strait was a last defence against the Romans in A.D. 61, but this did not in the end prevent the growth on both its flanks of a unified native culture, which in turn was an important focus for Celtic Christianity. Accessibility from the sea was again a dominant factor in attracting the Viking despoilers of the ecclesiastical settlements.

In parkland overlooking the Menai Strait at **Plas Newydd** (*519 697*) is a megalithic tomb consisting of a main chamber 3 m by 2.4 m and a smaller antechamber, each with its own capstone, but there is no mound or other feature to give cultural definition. Not far away is **Bryn yr Hen Bobl** (*519 690*), fully excavated in 1929. A kidney-shaped mound contains a simple chamber with funnel-shaped forecourt facing E. A notable feature is the revetted terrace 12 m wide extending

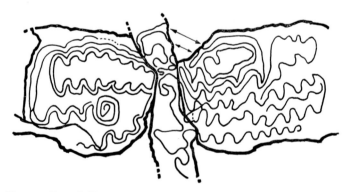

Figure 5. Bryn Celli Ddu (Area 2): a stone with meandering groove, found at the centre of the chambered cairn. Scale 1:20. *After R.C.A.M., Crown Copyright.*

100 m to the S., predating the cairn but integral with it. Earlier neolithic settlement material incorporated in the structure included stone
axes and pottery of plain 'western' and Peterborough types. The tomb
contained remains of at least twenty individuals.

Bryn Celli Ddu
Fig. 5; *PA* p. 55   *508 702* AN
A simple passage grave without side chambers, where full excavation in
1928 revealed a complicated sequence of construction. The single
polygonal chamber with a freestanding pillar inside, and the approach
passage, were covered by a mound nearly 50 m in diameter; but this was
a late phase, for the heavy stone kerb of the tomb was set in the partly
silted ditch of an earlier stone circle now thought to belong to the henge
monument tradition. The central element of the circle was a ritual pit,
beside which had stood a stone covered with meandering linear decoration. A small mound has been restored over the tomb. In State care;
apply at farmhouse for admission and pamphlet, weekdays and Sunday
afternoons.

The circular earthwork **Castell Bryngwyn** (*465 671*; in State care,
accessible at any time without charge) was a defensive earthwork 55 m in
diameter in its final form (I century A.D.), but it had been refashioned
from an earlier structure of neolithic date comparable to one of the
henge monuments at Llandegai (Area 6). Also probably in the henge
tradition, the *Bryngwyn Circle* (*462 669*), was supposed to have consisted
of nine stones inside a ditch with outer bank, but only two stones
remain, 3 and 4 m high.

Caer Leb
INV p. 103   *473 674* AN
An unusually sited defended settlement of the III century A.D. The low
position in a marshy area allowed water to fill the two ditches. A round
hut and a rectangular building were found inside by excavation. In
State care, accessible at any time without charge.

The route northwards *via* Llangefni passes **Maen Addwyn** (*461
833*), a standing stone over 3 m high, before passing over **Bodafon
Mountain**, where at *471 850* one of two homestead enclosures has
yielded III century A.D. Samian ware. In view to the N.W. is *Parys
Mountain* (*44 90*), where Roman copper mining has been proved. Cakes
of the metal, bearing official stamps and weighing up to 33 kg, have been
found in hut groups and elsewhere in Anglesey.

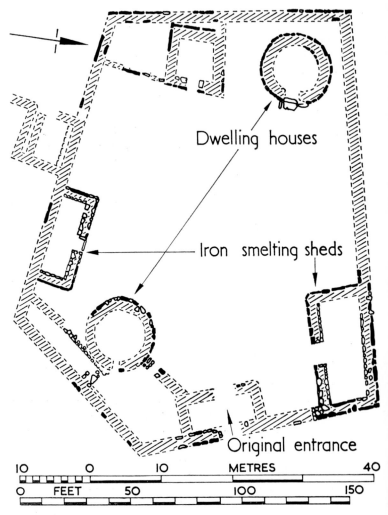

Dwelling houses

Iron smelting sheds

Original entrance

10   O   10   METRES   40

O   FEET   50   100   150

Figure 6. Din Lligwy (Area 2): an enclosed hut group of the IV century A.D. *After R.C.A.M., Crown Copyright.*

Din Lligwy

Fig. 6; *INV* p. 133   *496 862* AN

The two round huts used as living quarters are likely to have been part of
an open settlement of early Roman date, included in the strong pentagonal enclosure in the late IV century A.D. Six hearths in two of the
rectangular buildings show that they were used for iron workshops, but
one was a gatehouse. In State care, open always without charge.

Lligwy Burial Chamber

PA p. 52   *501 861* AN

The huge capstone rests on several stones and slabs inserted in a rock-
cut pit, which accounts for two-thirds of the 1.5 m height of the chamber. Pottery found in 1908 with the bones of thirty individuals shows
continuity of use from Neolithic to Early Bronze Age times, but detail
is lacking for comparative study of the tomb. In State care, open always
without charge. The same continuity was also apparent at **Pant-y-saer
Burial Chamber** (*509 824*), similarly sunk in a pit, but covered by an
oval mound along with its forecourt.

Pant-y-saer Hut Group

INV p. 70   *514 825* AN

In contrast with Din Lligwy, the strong enclosure wall is oval in plan,
and one of the two circular dwellings is integral with its construction.
Though rectilinear structures have been added, and some pottery
imitates Samian ware, the whole seems to belong to the post-Roman
phase, as indicated by a fine VI century silver penannular brooch.

Further native sites of the Roman period lie in the N.E. corner of the
island. **Bwrdd Arthur** (*585 815*), a hillfort of about 7 ha with overlapping entrance and rampart facing of large limestone slabs, is known
to have been extensively occupied in the IV century, though it may have
originated in pre-Roman times. In the **Deer Park** (*626 805*) at Penmon
is an extensive system of terraced fields and round huts, but no attempt
at defensive enclosure, implying perhaps an earlier date in the native
Iron Age.

Penmon was also an important centre of early Celtic Christianity,
founded by St. Seiriol in the VI century. The *Deer Park Cross* (*625 806*)
and *St. Seiriol's Well* (*632 808*) are probably replacements of structures
originating in earlier post-Roman centuries, though the cell attached to
the latter may be original. Both sites are in State care, accessible at any
time without charge.

THE LLEYN PENINSULA   82 km (51 miles)
AREA 3   Caernarvonshire CA
          Map 123; 1″ 115; 2½″ SH *12, 13, 22–24, 32–34, 43, 44*

Here is the Land's End of North Wales, offering all that this implies by
way of remoteness. The crossing to Bardsey is easily arranged by
enquiry in Aberdaron, but the mainland will suffice for most people
with limited time. Pwllheli has grown as a holiday resort on a market
town nucleus, and provides conventional accommodation, while the
motorist with initiative can find humble but hospitable lodgings in
many of the smaller villages, including the ancient borough of Nefyn
and the yachting centre of Abersoch.

   Like Anglesey and Pembrokeshire, the Lleyn Peninsula was always
open to seaborne influences, though their effect was not often very deep.
In the Iron Age successive colonising movements from the south and
east can be detected, matching the classic phases of southern Britain, but
absorbed on arrival by an indigenous population living in the characteristic stone-ramparted forts of the region.

Creigiau Gwineu
INV No. 1742   *228 274* CA
A small stone-ramparted fort, probably of pre-Roman date, the original
entrance being through a natural gully in the crags on the W. It overlooks an extensive system of celtic fields (*232 283 etc.*) overlaid with
medieval remains.

   Two sites on a hillside further west seem to represent differing
neolithic groups. At **Tanymuriau** (*238 288*) a long cairn has one
chamber of its original three preserved at the N.W. end, but its portal
entrance is obstructed by field walls. While this was the tomb of local
neolithic settlers, a group of specialist craftsmen were at work at the
Mynydd Rhiw Stone Axe Factory (*234 299*), quarrying a fine-grained
altered shale from pits up to 3.5 m deep. Tree-felling axes were made
for trading to the agricultural population, but more specialised tools
were made for their own use.

Castell Odo
INV No. 1472   *187 284* CA
Full excavation here has provided a basic sequence for the local Iron
Age. The first settlement, with pottery of Iron Age A type, was virtually

undefined. A double-banked ringwork was developed through some three centuries, ending with slighting by the Romans, though occupation of the round huts continued.

In view from Castell Odo is *Bardsey Island* (*12 22*), from early times renowned as the retreat and burial place of saints, but now favoured chiefly by artists and naturalists, and offering few visible remains. Closely connected with the early monastic tradition are two stones at **Cefnamwlch** (*234 353*) commemorating priests, one being stated to lie 'int he throng of brethren'. Both once stood at *Capel Anelog* (*156 274*), a simple rectangular structure 3.6 m wide. Also near the route northward is a *cromlech* on **Mynydd Cefnamwlch** (*230 345*), where three up-rights still support one capstone, while another lies close by.

The three great stone forts of Lleyn deserve detailed exploration, even if this adds a whole day to the present tour, since together they embody the whole sequence of native settlement from roots in the Bronze Age, through the adoption of communal defence for a scattered population, through the more concentrated grouping of dwellings allowed even under the Romans, down to the re-use of parts of the fortifications by early medieval rulers.

Garn Fadrun
INV No. 1650   *280 352* CA

Best approached from Garn village, involving a climb of 120 m up the S.E. slope. The inner enclosure of 5 ha is to be associated with the round hut foundations, ranging from 3 to 8 m in diameter, mostly concentrated on the N. and N.W. slopes outside. The outer rampart at each end encloses an area of 10.5 ha, including the ruins of the earlier ramparts, which were used as material for the construction of complexes of small subrectangular huts with attached compounds. The small summit fort is traditionally the 'castle of the sons of Owain' of XII century origin, though possibly earlier.

Garn Boduan
INV No. 1524   *310 393* CA

Best approached from the S., on B4354. Two main periods of forti-fication were both associated with internal round huts, of which there are about 170; the larger, second fort enclosed 14 ha. Both may be earlier than the second phase at Garn Fadrun. Finally the small summit fort produced datable material within the range II to VII century, so that its identification as the residence of Buan, an early VII century noble, is reasonable.

D

Plate 4. Tre'r Ceiri (Area 3): the most spectacular of the stone forts of Lleyn. *Photo: J. K. S. St. Joseph.*

Tre'r Ceiri

Pl. 4; *INV* No. 1056   *373 446* CA

Well named 'the town of the giants', and the best known of the Lleyn forts, it occupies the S.W. summit of Yr Eifl, whose triple peaks are often wrongly called The Rivals. In the same sequence as at Garn Fadrun, the main rampart enclosed round huts in its pre-Roman phase, which were adapted into subrectangular cells with the addition of others to a total of about 150 in Roman times. A second rampart was added on the N.W., and small enclosures extend outside on the S.W. also. The main rampart was not ruined between phases; indeed it stands to a height of 4 m in places, with sloping ramps for access on the inside. There are two well-preserved gateways at the S.W. end, one with a good terraced approach, and three smaller entrances. The summit is crowned by a large cairn, presumably of Bronze Age date.

Prominent on the skyline of **Mynydd Carnguwch** (*374 429*) is a large oval cairn, spread to a maximum of 40 m diameter. Its firmly revetted core has occasioned interpretations varying from medieval castle-mound to Iron Age mausoleum, but it is likely to be simply a case of Bronze Age 'one-upmanship'.

A final detour to the E. leads through an area of agricultural settlement probably bridging the Roman conquest. The lane cuts in half an enclosed hut-group at **Llain-llan** (*407 450*) and passes an isolated round hut 90 m to the E. with good orthostatic facing. A further walk leads through 6 ha of terraced fields, with a ruined hut-group near **Tyddyn-mawr** (*427 451*), to **Pen-y-gaer** (*429 455*). Here a stone wall up to 4.5 m thick encloses a dozen round hut platforms.

Carn Pentyrch
INV No. 1262   *424 418* CA
A further example of the re-use of an Iron Age hillfort (in this case with a single bank and ditch) as the site for a post-Roman stone-walled enclosure, so dated by similarity of construction to the summit fort at Garn Boduan. Features include a battered facing and projecting steps for access to the rampart top.

SNOWDON SOUTH   64 km (40 miles)
AREA 4   Caernarvonshire CA
    Map 115, 123, 124; 1″ 107, 115, 116; 2½″ SH *43, 44, 53, 54, 64, 65*

The south side of the Snowdon massif is a favourite haunt of those who want the best of the mountains and the coast at the same time. Portmadoc has exchanged the XIX century prosperity of the slate exporting industry for the present-day holiday harvest. Criccieth is an attractive alternative centre; also Beddgelert and the Gwynant Valley deep in the mountains.

Southern Snowdonia and the Merionethshire coast (Areas 18, 19) have much in common geographically and historically, with no serious interruption by the wide Dwyryd estuary. The main cultural changes of the British Iron Age rarely had more than a delayed and indirect influence on the Celtic unity established here in pre-Roman times. The foothills of Snowdon, however, form a link with the more progressive culture of Anglesey and the north coast (Areas 2, 5, 6).

Rhoslan Cromlech
INV No. 1377   *483 409* CA

The bare but massive bones of a megalithic tomb, of which the complete original form can only be guessed. *Coetan Arthur (499 413)*, though fragmentary and difficult of access, is more readily put in its cultural place in the passage grave tradition.

The course of the Roman road on its final approach to Segontium (Area 5) from the south was debatable before the auxiliary fort was revealed by gravel digging at *Pen Llystyn (481 449*; Fig. 12). Thorough examination during its destruction has provided the most complete plan of a timber fort in Wales. It was about 1.6 ha in area, built *c.* A.D. 80 for a mixed contingent of infantry and cavalry engaged in the conquest of north Wales, but soon abandoned and replaced by one only a quarter the size, also short-lived.

Llystyn Gwyn Inscribed Stone
INV No. 1016   *482 455* CA

A large boulder now set up in the farmyard once stood over the VI century grave of Icorix, son of Potentinus, as recorded in ogam symbols on one edge as well as in Latin on the face.

Remote on *Mynydd Craig-goch (500 477)* are three groups of huts and enclosures clearly of the Roman period type seen at Garn Fadrun and Tre'r Ceiri (Area 3), but here at 300–400 m above sea level they needed no defence. Even more remote are the mountain-top cairns like those on *Craig Cwm Silyn (525 502)* and *Moel Hebog (565 469)* built, one may suppose, in the most prominent positions for the leaders of Bronze Age nomadic pastoralists.

Usually in lower positions by streams are the open-air hearths where Bronze Age hunters cooked their game. They can be recognised by the U-shaped bank of heat-shattered stones thrown up around a trough, where they were used to boil water diverted from a stream. Five good examples are grouped near **Cefn Trefor-isaf** *(486 460)*.

Garndolbenmaen Round Hut
INV No. 977   *500 440* CA

An isolated Iron Age dwelling 8 m in diameter, with an entrance 2 m wide leading from a yard of similar size. The low wall which carried the conical roof is built of rubble packed between flat-faced boulders.

Castell Caerau
INV No. 924   *509 439* CA
The disproportionately strong wall of this little fort on a rocky eminence
is built largely of long blocks stacked as 'headers', and stands over 1 m
high in places. There is just enough room for a family unit to have
lived between the outcrops inside, though no huts remain. A similar
fort on **Craig y Tyddyn** (*506 427*) is not much bigger, but is built of
poorer material.

Braich y Gornel Hut Group
INV No. 937   *552 446* CA
Two round huts about 5 m in diameter with a small yard between formed
the nucleus of a farm unit of about 1.6 ha. Excavation produced no
datable relics, but unenclosed groups of this kind with a few enclosures
attached can reasonably be assumed to have originated in the pre-Roman
Iron Age. The lower slopes of this valley and of Cwm Pennant to the
N.W. are rich in these small farms, often covering large areas as at
Ceunant y Ddol (*548 460*) and *Caerfadog-uchaf* (*545 447*).
    The Glaslyn valley, leading deep into the mountains to the foot of
Snowdon itself, has many scattered settlements to compare with those
already sampled, but generally hard to find. Within reach is **Pen y
Gaer** (*586 457*), a larger version of Castell Caerau; also **Muriau'r-dre**
(*655 541*), a good group of unenclosed huts.

Dinas Emrys
INV No. 742   *606 492* CA
Now best approached up the N.E. ridge, but with its original entrance
through two main ramparts and several lines of natural crag at the W.
The remains are not substantial (apart from a XII century A.D. tower),
but interest centres on excavation results in the area around an artificial
pool near the centre. After initial pre-Roman occupation, the pool was
built to supply a I or II century A.D. settlement which continued into
the V century, thus reaching a possible date for the legendary activities
of Vortigern against Emrys (Ambrosius Aurelianus), involving witch-
craft.

SNOWDON NORTH   76 km (47 miles)
AREA 5   Caernarvonshire CA
              Map 115, 1″ 107, 115; 2½″ SH *44–46, 55, 56*

The quarry village of Llanberis lies at the deepest penetration of the
Snowdon block of mountains, where now its tourist trade relies on the
ease of access by rack railway to the summit of Eryri. Hotels abound
here, but Caernarvon is well enough provided and must take pride of
place as an exciting place to stay. The premier castle of Wales stands as
the symbol of an uneasy English domination for seven hundred years;
now familiar to the world in a ceremonial role, with its fortified town it
deserves a whole day's visit to itself. The lingering air of a once busy
port here and at Port Dinorwic is a reminder of the vital role of sea
communications in earlier times for both the English and the Roman
military regimes, and less consciously for the development of the Celtic
settlement pattern which dominates the archaeological scene. The hills
up to 250 m above sea level are good hunting ground for hut groups and
systems of early agricultural enclosures, many of which have been little
disturbed by modern progressive farming.

Dinas Dinorwig
INV No. 1170   *550 653* CA
A fortification in a key position, not greatly elevated but overlooking the
main line of communication towards the north coast from Segontium.
An earlier stone-faced rampart, with two simple gaps for entrances, is
possibly quite early in the pre-Roman period. It was entirely enclosed
in a double defence of banks and ditches, with a single entrance and a
sizable annexe, in an intrusive style to be ascribed to immigrants of
Iron Age B origin not long before the Roman conquest, at which time
it is likely to have fallen into disuse.

Hafoty Wern-las Huts and Fields
Fig. 7; *INV* No. 1340   *501 582* CA
In an extensive area of terraces are three distinct types of domestic
structure. The best preserved, and clearly the latest on the evidence of
II-IV century A.D. pottery, is a straight-sided enclosed group closely
comparable to Din Lligwy (Area 2), with a rectangular smithy in one
corner. The round hut within could have been re-used from the earlier
unenclosed group, of which four more lie outside to the N. Nearby on

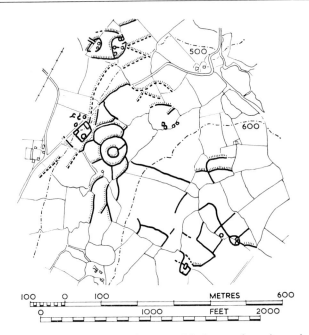

Figure 7. Hafoty Wern-las (Area 5): traces of the layout of a native agricultural community of the Roman period. *After R.C.A.M., Crown Copyright.*

the S.E. is a double circular terrace which is probably a 'concentric' like Llwyndu-bach (below) without its central hut, perhaps contemporary with the unenclosed group.

A generally similar area of hut-groups and fields lies S. of **Rhostryfan** (*494 572 &c*). On lower ground to the S.W. at **Llwyndu-bach** (*479 540*) is an excavated example of the 'triple-concentric enclosure' type of homestead found also in Merionethshire (Area 18). The dwelling house at the centre was of two periods, each with a central hearth and roof supports for the 9 m diameter. The intermediate circle formed a yard 26 m across, while the outer one, presumably for cattle, was about 60 m in diameter. A I century A.D. date is probable.

Caerau Hut-Groups and Fields
INV Nos. 826–834   *469 489* CA
Easily accessible, incorporating both oval and rectilinear types of group

among terraced fields. Excavation of the largest group gave a date in the II and III centuries A.D.

Cefn Graeanog Cairn and Stone
INV No. 855   *455 492* CA
An impressive monolith 3 m high marks the site of a Bronze Age cairn, which has seven visible kerbstones beyond a field wall. A similar standing stone near *Glynllifon* (*445 541*) marked a burial accompanied by a plain, early type of cinerary urn.

Bachwen Burial Chamber
INV No. 861   *407 495* CA
A freestanding chamber with three original supporters, notable for the array of about 110 cupmarks on the upper surface of the capstone, which is thus likely to have been exposed in antiquity.

Craig y Dinas
INV No. 1281   *448 520* CA
Sited on a low spur in a river bend, with two periods of stone building in the defences combined with earth ramparts and ditches. Probably of similar date to Dinas Dinorwig (above), entirely pre-Roman.

Dinas Dinlle
INV No. 1211   *437 563* CA
Two massive banks have been thrown up round a glacial hill now being eroded by the sea. Its form and position immediately suggest a beach-head fortification of Iron Age B immigrants, though the only finds have belonged to II and III century A.D. occupation.

Segontium
Fig. 12; *INV* No. 1127; *RFW* p. 59   *485 624* CA
The Roman auxiliary fort established at the north-west corner of the military road system of Wales at the time of Agricola's punitive conquest (A.D. 78) was repeatedly abandoned and rebuilt, depending on current military needs both locally and elsewhere in Britain. This history as revealed by excavation is fully explained in the booklet available at the **Museum** on the site, where the stone foundations of various phases are open to view during standard hours. Also in Caernarvon is the III century walled fort of **Hen Waliau** (*482 624*), probably a storage depot for Segontium. A portion of the wall is to be seen in gardens by the A499 road. In the museum note a *milestone*,

found at *566 636*, where the Roman road from Segontium would have branched to the S.W. and N.W. The name of the Emperor Traianus Decius gives it a date A.D. 249–51. The fort site is in State care, open during regulated hours.

THE OGWEN   29 km (18 miles)
AREA 6   Caernarvonshire CA
                    Map 115; 1″ 107; 2½″ SH *56, 57, 66, 67, 77*

The Celtic monastic centre at Bangor has appropriately developed through a medieval cathedral town to its modern successor as a university town. It is a natural focus of tourism and commerce, a link between the Liverpool-dominated north coast and the interior of the ancient

Plate 5. Llandegai Henge Monuments (Area 6): cropmarks which led to the discovery of two good examples of neolithic ritual sites. *Photo: J. K. S. St. Joseph.*

Gwynedd. It serves well for archaeological exploration in all directions, and its **Museum of Welsh Antiquities** in College Road (*579 724*) offers a wide-ranging collection of material from the area, which will give added meaning to many of the sites to be visited in Anglesey and Caernarvonshire. There is also a fine array of Welsh by-gones and porcelain. (Hours of opening are 10.00 to 16.00 on weekdays, but only 13.00 to 16.00 November to March, and closed on Bank Holidays.)

The present-day character of the Ogwen valley as seen by the casual visitor has been determined by recent history, for Bethesda and its slate quarries dominate everything from architecture to unemployment. The whole of the low plateau between the rivers Ogwen and Cegin, capped with glacial outwash gravels from the Snowdon ice cap, was an attraction for immigrant settlers as soon as it became habitable in post-glacial times, being at a natural meeting point of coastal communications by land and sea. A neolithic site of primary importance, now covered by factory buildings, was discovered on this plateau by aerial photography at *Llandegai* (*594 712*; Plate 5). Rescue excavation proved the two large circles to be the ditches of 'henge monuments' dated by radiocarbon to *c.* 2650 and 1850 B.C., the ceremonial and burial sites of people probably of distant mesolithic ancestry rather than immigrant farmers of the tomb-building cultures. To the latter can be attributed traces of rectangular houses in the same field dated to *c.* 3300 B.C.

There is only a narrow strip of coastal plain east of the mouth of the Ogwen, but the lower slopes of its valley and of the smaller valleys of the Anafon and Afon Ddu bear ample evidence of early settlement from Bronze Age to medieval times, making this an area particularly rewarding for exploration at length. Behind Llanfairfechan nine scattered huts up to 8.5 m in diameter at **Gwern-y-plas** (*686 748*) have some good walling preserved, while the much ruined small hillfort of **Dinas** (*700 738*) has huts of similar size, built when the need for defence had passed, perhaps under Roman rule. The **Roman road** from the Conwy valley descends from the mountain not far to the south (Fig. 12), well authenticated by three milestones. A good area of cultivation terraces of the same period lies on the W. slope of **Garreg Fawr** (*685 733*).

Maes y Gaer
INV No. 12   *663 725* CA
A stone-built hillfort of the pre-Roman Iron Age, with an entrance passage 3.4 m wide lengthened out to 6 m in a rampart that is often less than 3 m thick. This was apparently a refuge hillfort, having no hut foundations visible.

Hafod Gelyn Homestead
INV No. 31   *675 714* CA

A fair example of a rectilinear enclosure with two round hut foundations, presumably a native farmstead of Roman date. The rectangular house foundation on the N. over a third round hut site suggests continued use into post-Roman times. The terraced fields on the slope above seem to belong primarily to the oval hut-group at *677 716* on **Foel Dduarth** and another at *Bod-Silin* (*677 723*), both possibly of earlier date. At two places on the S. side of the **Anafon valley** are detached round-huts, typical of many that have no elaborate field systems (*684 711 &*
678 710).

Carnedd y Saeson
INV No. 67   *678 717* CA

One of a group of seven Bronze Age cairns, of particular interest for its retaining circle and inner circle of slabs on edge. One side stone and the capstone of the central cist are visible. Similar elements survive in **two cairns** at *674 716* among the field terraces.

Llanllechid Hut Group
INV No. 494   *632 687* CA

Three round huts line the S. wall of an oval enclosure 36 m by 24 m, terraced to 3 m high above a stream. The facing of boulders is typical of the walls of several groups which are scattered among the field system to the S. and W.

Moel Faban Huts and Fields
INV No. 519   *637 681* CA

Higher on the mountain slopes are groups of enclosures with dispersed huts, mainly grouped at their junctions. While cultivation is suggested by the terracing of the smaller fields, the larger ones are presumably pastoral enclosures. The hut walls are of well-laid stone here, but the single huts in a pastoral group further up **Cwm Ffrydlas** (*644 684*) consist only of roughly piled stone. Some of the stone heaps in both groups may be Bronze Age cairns; there is, however, no doubt about those on the summit of *Moel Faban*, one of which (*635 682*) yielded a cinerary urn to early excavators. The remote peaks of *Carnedd Dafydd* (*633 630*), *Carnedd Llywelyn* (*683 644*) and *Drosgl* (*663 680*) all have their cairns, but they are inevitably mutilated.

2 NORTHERN RIVERS
The Conwy and Clwyd

Figure 8. Dinorben (Area 9): handle mount from a bucket of the Roman period. Full size. *Drawing: National Museum of Wales.*

THE LOWER CONWY
AREA 7

58 km (36 miles)
Caernarvonshire CA, Denbighshire DE
Map 115; 1" 107; 2½" SH 76–78, 87, 88

The immediate impact of Conway is one of medieval solidarity, a vital protection for the supply lines of an occupying power. The great drums of the castle towers now loom over three bridges, of which Telford's masterpiece of suspension is sadly sandwiched but happily preserved. Llandudno and its satellites offer a better choice of lodgings and hotels.

The limestone hills of the Great Orme peninsula and the sheltered river mouth presented an open invitation to neolithic immigrants in search of cultivable land and good grazing. The river itself, on the other hand, seems to have become a barrier to coastwise cultural movement by Iron Age times, to judge from the differences of hillfort architecture on either side.

Lletty'r Filiast
INV No. 378   *772 829* CA
The polygonal chamber has four supporters remaining, but part of the capstone has been broken away. The mound has been greatly robbed, leaving what is basically a rock outcrop, which gives little idea of the original shape of this neolithic chambered cairn.

Allor Moloch
PRRD p. 354   *793 747* DE
The rectangular chamber of a megalithic tomb with a massive capstone and a pair of uprights forming a portal at the S.E. There is no trace of a

cairn, but the siting on a rocky tongue achieves the effect of a long mound.

Caerhun Roman Fort

INV No. 166; *RFW* p. 56   *776 704* CA

The fort of Kanovium was built in timber in the late I century A.D. and rebuilt in stone *c.* 150. After destruction in *c.* 200 there was spasmodic occupation only. The N.E. quarter of the fort is covered by the church-yard, but the remainder was excavated fully in 1926–9. A bath house was found outside the fort on the E., while a jetty and dock at the riverside emphasise the soundness of this strategic position, set up as a bridgehead in hostile territory.

The *Roman road* from Segontium (Area 5) to Caerhun approached the Conwy valley by a moorland route (Fig. 12) ignored for modern traffic, and can be followed on foot for several km on either side of **Bwlch y Ddeufaen**. The two standing stones at *715 718* which give the pass its name are the most westerly of a series of monuments which suggest a prehistoric origin for the route.

Cerrig Pryfaid Circle

INV No. 177   *724 713* CA

Of the 10 stones remaining at a minimum spacing of 3 m only half are over 0.5 m high. Outliers on the W. further distinguish this apparently ceremonial site of the Bronze Age from the nearby burial cairn **Barclo-diad y Gawres** (*716 716*), which has an eccentrically placed cist as large in area as the chambers of many neolithic tombs. Further E. along the lane are two isolated **standing stones** at *736 716* and *738 717*, the latter being called *Ffon y Cawr* (The Giant's Stick).

Maen y Bardd

INV No. 178   *740 718* CA

A capstone 2 m long, four supporters and a fifth sidestone make up the well-preserved megalithic chamber of a much denuded cairn. It may be a coincidence that two further *standing stones* (*742 718*) are aligned on this cromlech.

Iron Age settlement on the W. slope of the valley is represented by an area of *lynchetted fields* S.W. and N.E. of Maen y Bardd (*739 716* and *742 720*), but hut groups are not well preserved. **Caer Bach** (*744 730*) is a small round fortification where an inner stone wall 3 m thick and an outer bank and ditch suggest continued occupation through a change of style in fortification.

Plate 6. Conway Mountain (Area 7): the foundations of one of the round huts in the pre-Roman hillfort. *Photo: R.C.A.M., Crown Copyright.*

Pen y Gaer
INV No. 315   *750 693* CA
One of the most interesting hillforts of Caernarvonshire, in which the earlier, stone-ramparted enclosure was further protected by two areas of *chevaux-de-frise* on the W. and S., consisting of pointed stones set on end to foil a frontal attack, a device of foreign origin found in South Wales also (see Areas 39, 41, 42). The strengthening of the S. side with two banks and ditches indicates the arrival of new ideas in defence, seen in three forts in Area 5. Excavation revealed iron-working in one of the 20 huts inside and between the ramparts.

Conway Mountain Hillfort
Pl. 6; *INV* No. 201   *760 778* CA
An Iron Age stone-walled fort exhibiting the orthostatic rampart facing typical of many in Caernarvonshire, and containing about 60 round hut foundations. The W. end was strongly refortified, still in pre-Roman times, with extra defences and new huts. Excavation in 1951 revealed much interesting constructional detail, but poor domestic equipment.

By contrast the large hillfort of *Braich y Ddinas* 6 km to the W. (*701 753*), now entirely quarried away, contained about 90 huts which were occupied entirely in the Roman period, indicating a surprisingly lenient colonial policy.

The Druids' Circle
INV No. 277   *723 746* CA
The best of a group of Bronze Age circles on the level moorland edge, reached by a stiff climb from Penmaen-mawr. Ten stones up to 2 m high still stand in a low bank around an almost circular area 26 m in diameter, with a gap 2 m wide on the W. Primary and secondary cremation burials of children suggest a ritual function for the monument, which was built beside a trackway apparently already in use.

Cors y Carneddau Cairn
INV No. 425   *716 747* CA
A large stony mound 19 m in diameter, one of a group of four cairns. The remains of a surrounding ditch and bank suggest the classic bell-

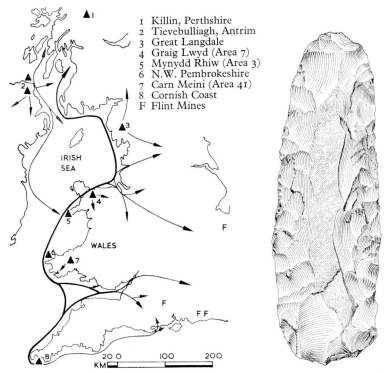

1 Killin, Perthshire
2 Tievebulliagh, Antrim
3 Great Langdale
4 Graig Lwyd (Area 7)
5 Mynydd Rhiw (Area 3)
6 N.W. Pembrokeshire
7 Carn Meini (Area 41)
8 Cornish Coast
F Flint Mines

IRISH SEA

WALES

20 0   100   200
KM

Figure 9. Graig Lwyd (Area 7): sources of stone axes for the neolithic coastal trade; and an axe in roughout form. Scale 1:3

barrow form of the Wessex Culture, making it a burial monument broadly contemporary with the ritual Druids' Circle nearby. More typical of the area are the smaller stone-kerbed cairns of about 10 m diameter with central slab-lined cists on *Foel Lwyd* (*713 727*) and *Bryniau Bugeilydd* (*720 739*). However, the mountain-top cairns *Carnedd y Ddelw* (*708 705*), with its legend of the find of a 'gold image', and *Carnedd Penyborth-goch* (*708 696*) are also prominent enough to belong to the wealthy traders whose route to Ireland skirted these uplands.

Graig Lwyd Axe Factory
Fig. 9; *INV* Vol. I, p. xli   *717 750* CA
The outcrops and screes at the E. end of Penmaenmawr Mountain are famous as one of the sources of material exploited by neolithic man for his stone axes. The best deposits of waste material have now been removed by quarrying, but excavations in 1920 provided ample information on the technology of flaking this tough stone into roughouts for trading to distant parts of Britain, where the final grinding and polishing were done. Smaller outcrops of the same rock at Dinas and Garreg Fawr (Area 6), and different rock sources in other parts of western Britain, were all exploited by these axe specialists who used the sea as much as land for their journeys.

Rapallo House Museum
Fferm Bach Rd., Llandudno   *794 815* CA
A museum affiliated to the National Museum of Wales, based on a private collection covering a wide range of interests. It contains many casual finds of local origin as well as excavated material from Caerhun Roman fort.

In St. Mary's Church nearby (*793 803*) an **inscribed stone**, assigned to *c.* A.D. 500, commemorates 'Sanctinus the Priest. (May he rest) in peace.'

THE UPPER CONWY   21 km (13 miles)
AREA 8   Caernarvonshire CA, Denbighshire DE
                                Map 115, 116; 1″ 107; 2½″ SH 65, 75, 85

The headwaters of the Conwy and of its tributaries the Llugwy and the

Lledr lie deep in the Snowdon massif, an area of high rainfall today and equally inhospitable in antiquity except for pastoralists. There are consequently few sites to include in the itinerary for this area, but the scenic wealth is unbounded, and is well worth a brief stay at Betws-y-coed or in one of the forested valleys radiating from it, where there are excellent hotels and guest houses.

Capel Garmon Chambered Tomb
PRRD p. 323   *818 543* DE

A well-preserved tomb, which yielded interesting constructional detail when it was thoroughly examined in 1924. A false portal in the E. end, between the rounded horns of a long cairn, and a double chamber entered by a passage from its side indicate affinity with the Severn-

Plate 7. Penmachno (Area 8): one of the early Christian memorials preserved at the church *Photo: R.C.A.M., Crown Copyright.*

E

Cotswold tombs, in spite of geographical separation from the nearest members of that group in South Wales (Areas 26, 28, 31, 35). This is confirmed by features such as the extensive use of dry-stone revetment, covered all round by added cairn material, and corbelling of the chambers inwards. As in some other megalithic tombs, beaker pottery shows that use continued after the Neolithic period. In State care, open always without charge. A pamphlet is available.

The Bronze Age is much in evidence on the E. side of the Conwy above Llanrwst, though mainly in finds from burial sites that have been disturbed. Presumably also of Bronze Age date are the alignments of small stones at *Hafod y Garreg* (*878 535*), where only one row remains, and *Hafod y Dre* (*885 537*), where two rows remain of the sixteen recorded in 1884.

Penmachno Inscribed Stones
INV No. 646   *790 506* CA
A minor tributary valley of the Conwy leads to Penmachno, where three of the five early Christian stones in the church are noteworthy for their informative inscriptions. The 'heap of stones' in which Carausius lies (Plate 7) is a formula rather than fact. 'Cantiorix, citizen of Venedos, cousin of Maglus the magistrate' indicates the persistence of a Roman pattern of government. The stone of the son of Avitorius, set up 'in the time of Justinus' the Consul, is closely datable to *c.* 540.

The Roman road from Caerhun (Area 7) southwards kept mainly to the hills, but where it dipped across the Llugwy valley at *Bryn y Gefeiliau* (*746 572*) a minor fort was set up in the I century, possibly as a mining station. (Fig. 12.)

THE ELWY   64 km (40 miles)
AREA 9   Denbighshire DE
           Map 116; 1″ 107, 108; 2½″ SH 86, 87, 96, 97, SJ 06, 07

The inland area drained by the Elwy into the Clwyd contains few prehistoric sites other than Bronze Age barrows, mostly difficult to reach among the forestry plantations that have given a new character to much of the former moorland. In contrast the coastal zone of hills 10 km broad between the Conwy and Clwyd is now, as in antiquity, more attractive for agricultural settlement. A central sector of limestone formations is of particular interest for its caves and hillforts, which have cultural affinity with the eastern flank of the Clwyd, but are better visited from Colwyn Bay or some other convenient point on this holiday coast. Denbigh would be a pleasant alternative, from which the short tour of Area 10 could also be undertaken.

Pen y Corddin

Pl. 8; *PRRD* p. 29   *915 764* DE

Sited on an isolated limestone mass, so bound by precipitous cliffs on nearly every side that strong artificial defences were needed only against approach from the north. The main enclosure of 10 ha is defined by two stone-revetted ramparts 12 m apart, with no ditch between, while the

Plate 8. Pen y Corddin (Area 9): one of the largest and strongest hillforts of the Iron Age in north Wales. *Photo: J. K. S. St. Joseph.*

single rampart of the outer enclosure added a further 5 ha. The three entrances of the main enclosure were sited at the heads of gullies with the ramparts turned inwards, those at the N.W. and N.E. being lengthened to form passages flanked by guard chambers at their inner ends. A small postern in the E. side gave access by a steep path to a spring below. Several hut sites can be seen from the air, but are hard to locate on the ground. Excavation revealed many structural details of ramparts and gateways; though the few datable finds were all of Roman date the original fort was probably earlier. The similarly strong fort of **Castell Cawr** (*936 767*) is smaller and less accessible, but has some good walling and an inturned entrance.

Dinorben
DIN   *968 757* DE
The best known hillfort of the north coast, since it was thoroughly excavated in 1912–22 and periodically since 1955 in advance of quarrying, which will destroy it entirely in the end. A triangular area of only 2 ha was enclosed by limestone cliffs on two sides and by a massive defence system on the S., which in the last three of six occupation phases consisted of a huge sloping-faced rampart with two smaller ones outside. The main entrance at the S.E. was modified several times, to be seen now as a stone-faced passage over 10 m long, with guard chambers at the inner end. Many hut floors were found when topsoil was stripped, apparently belonging to all phases; though dating evidence was scanty, this fort is thought to have originated in pre-Roman times, continuing in use after the conquest as a native settlement of some importance. Finds included III and IV century A.D. pottery and coins, and two bronze bucket-handle mountings decorated with ox-heads in a derived Celtic style (Fig. 8).

Tyddyn Bleiddyn Long Cairn
PRRD p. 64   *007 724* DE
Now suffering from neglect, so that of the two chambers found in early excavations only the northern one can be made out. It was 4.5 m long including a short passage, lying crosswise in the end of a cairn 20 m long by 8 m wide, and contained the skeletal remains of at least 12 individuals of all ages, but no distinctive cultural evidence. The other chamber was similarly placed further S., with many more burials.

The limestone cliffs on the N. of the Elwy before it turns north towards the sea contain caves which have yielded traces of human occupation of palaeolithic date. At *Bont Newydd* (*015 710*) were a few crude quartzite implements and a human tooth, and at *Cefn* (*020 710*) one of four caves open to the public contained a human skull, jaw and limb bones, and some flint flakes.

Of the several Bronze Age burial mounds in the farm and park land on the gently undulating western flank of the Clwyd, none is both well preserved and easily accessible. One at *Plas Heaton* (*033 686*) was the site of a productive excavation as early as 1850, when a crouched skeleton was found in a primary burial cist, with a beaker covered all over with finger-nail impressions. Another group of barrows lies on the higher ridges flanking the Aled S. of Llansannan, the most accessible being four at **Rhos Domen** (*900 640*).

Gwytherin Stones
ECMW No. 177   *877 614* DE
Four stones about 1 m high stand in line in the churchyard at a regular 2 m spacing. While a prehistoric origin for the alignment is possible, their chief interest lies in the inscription on the most westerly one, which commemorates one Vinnemaglus son of Senemaglus. Two stones in **Llangernyw churchyard** (*875 674*) bearing crosses of VII–IX century character are more likely to have been originally intended for the head and foot of a burial.

THE UPPER CLWYD   40 km (25 miles)
AREA 10   Denbighshire DE, Merioneth ME
                            Map 116; 1″ 108; 2½″ SJ *04, 05, 15, 16*

The part-forested moorland in which the south-western tributaries of the Clwyd rise is properly a continuation of the Elwy basin (Area 9), but as the streams cut more deeply towards their convergence near Ruthin, they provide sharp relief as raw material for the defended settlements of Iron Age agriculturalists. To the E. lie the southernmost of the great hillforts of the Clwydian Hills, allied in character to those of Areas 11 and 12. Ruthin is the natural centre of the area, but Denbigh would serve equally well for a combined tour with Area 9.

Foel Fenlli
PRRD p. 183   *163 601* DE
A fort of some 10 ha on one of the highest summits of the Clwydian

Hills (over 500 m). The ramparts, which closely follow the contours, are single, double or triple as demanded by the steepness of the natural slope. The entrance at the W. end is of the inturned type. Excavations in 1849 showed that occupation continued from pre-Roman into Roman times. **Moel y Gaer** (*149 617*) is less than half as big but of similar contour form. There were originally two ramparts all around, and a third across the level ground to the N.E. guarding one of the two inturned entrances, but they are poorly preserved in places.

In passing through Ruthin one may perhaps allow time to find **Maen Huail** (*123 582*) on the W. side of the Market Square. It is no more than a plain boulder, but legend states that on it King Arthur beheaded Huail, brother of Gildas the historian of those times.

Craig Adwywynt
PRRD p. 213   *122 544* DE
Away from the Clwydian Hills now, south of Ruthin, the hillforts assume a rather different character, adapted to more intricate topography. Here a narrow ridge, reached by a steep farm track from the W., is naturally strong on that side, but has the ruins of a single stone rampart on the E. and an extra one across the ridge at the S. end. The damaged entrance at the N.E. included an inturn of the rampart and a protective outwork.

Dinas Melin-y-wig
HM p. 135   *049 491* ME
Sited in farm land on a promontory in a bend of the River Clwyd, this contour fort of over 5 ha has a striking succession of three banks and ditches giving great defensive depth. In contrast is the undefended Iron Age settlement of which fragments are preserved in a forest clearing at **Cefn Bannog** (*018 510*), with only three huts up to 10 m in diameter remaining of the several once visible.

The Bronze Age sites of the Upper Clwyd area, consisting as they do of cairns and circles on open, relatively high ground, have suffered in the recent creation of reservoirs and the development of Clocaenog Forest. At **Capel Hiraethog** (*032 545*) only one circle is satisfactorily preserved out of a group of three, and that only has three of the 19 stones which stood in a circle of about 20 m diameter with a small central mound.

THE LOWER CLWYD   63 km (39 miles)
AREA 11   Flintshire FL
                    Map 116; 1″ 108; 2½″ SJ *06–08, 16, 17*

The sprawl of caravans and other manifestations of leisure for urban thousands have stifled the natural assets of Rhyl and the coastal plain. For those who want lodging in more sedate surroundings there is a limited choice in the miniature cathedral city of St. Asaph; here too is a small collection of local finds housed in the Diocesan Office by the Close, open only by request.

The elevated and gently undulating country between the Clwyd and the estuary of the Dee has provided a more continuous record of prehistoric settlement than many other parts of Wales, owing mainly to the underlying geology. The limestone offered caves for Stone Age habitation and burial, while the light soil and vegetation favoured game and early agriculture. Grazing would have been good in both Bronze and Iron Ages, and for the Romans there was a ready source of lead at both sides of the area.

Facing south and overlooking a small stream in a side valley of the main Clwyd escarpment, the two adjacent caves of *Ffynnon Beuno* and *Cae Gwyn (085 724)* are key sites for the palaeolithic succession in Britain. From excavations in both in the 1880s came tools of early Aurignacian type, clearly sealed at Cae Gwyn by glacial drift which had been deposited by the final advance of the northern ice sheet.

Important neolithic sites excavated in 1912–14 on the rock of *Dyserth Castle (060 799)* and at *King Charles' Bowling Green (071 815)* were the farm settlements of people who were probably distinct from the elusive axe traders of the western sea routes whose wares they used. Notably absent are the megalithic chambered tombs one might expect in the area, but exactly the same purpose of communal burial was served by using caves. A rockshelter on the S. side of the *Gop* hill *(086 801)* contained a walled-in space about 1.5 m square in which the remains of 14 individuals were found, with objects of neolithic and Bronze Age date. In side passages of the adjacent *North-west Cave* were six more skeletons, possibly reinterred from elsewhere.

The Gop Cairn
Pl. 9; *PRRF* p. 156   *086 801* FL
This is surely the most imposing mound in Wales, though its apparent size is partly due to its position. The overall height of 12 m and the

Plate 9. The Gop Cairn (Area 11): the largest Bronze Age cairn in Wales, with the Gop Caves just down the slope on the left. *Photo: J. K. S. St. Joseph.*

maximum diameter of 100 m no doubt conceal a natural core formed by the hilltop. A vertical shaft in 1886 and two galleries failed to reveal any central features, disclosing only a few animal bones. The Gop Cairn's size invites comparison with the Boyne chambered tombs, but it may be in reality the most important of the many Bronze Age burial mounds of the region, indicating wealth or status such as might accrue from participation in the metal trade with Ireland along the north coast.

A startling example of such wealth came to light in 1815 in a small quarry at *Bryn Sion (135 719)*, though it took the keen eye of a gipsy to recognise its value. Used for a while as a gate fastening, it proved in the end to be a gold torc, a twisted rectangular bar of metal bent into a hoop.

Of the smaller burial mounds not many are worth special visits, lying as they do in enclosed ground where they are liable to reduction by ploughing. Good, accessible examples are two at **Brynyrorsedd** (*076 812*) and **Bryndigrif** (*127 792*) on the N. side of the B5332 road, while of the dozen or so well-preserved examples S.W. and W. of Holywell those at **Gorsedd** (*149 766*) deserve mention. Many have suffered damage from early, though no doubt well-intentioned, excavations, for which the survival of pottery and other finds in museums is hardly adequate compensation.

Two excavations were more successful. At **Pantydulath** (*096 764*) in 1957 a small primary cairn covered a central tree-trunk coffin containing a child's skeleton, but no grave goods; also an eccentric pit with a cremation in an inverted urn. The cairn was enlarged in two stages, incorporating a stone ring and kerb. At **Ffrith y Garreg-wen** (*136 759*) also the cairn had been twice enlarged. In the primary cairn was an imperfect cremation in a natural hollow, with a stone pendant and flints. Two secondary cremations followed, one with an urn and a flat copper dagger. The third stage contained five cremations with pottery fragments.

Two other mounds were examined in relation to Offa's Dyke in 1925. One at *Brynbella* (*130 771*) was thought, but not proved, to be sepulchral. The other on **Holywell Racecourse** (*152 753*) had an early Bronze Age inhumation in a pit, surrounded by a circular trench of ritual purpose. An embanked oval enclosure eccentrically placed round the barrow was also certainly earlier than the dyke.

Offa's Dyke

Fig. 12; *OD* p. 5   *083 799* etc. FL

Although the intended course of this great boundary earthwork of the Mercian kingdom is known, it was never completed between the Dee and Severn, so that there are few well-preserved sections in Area II. The B5332 road follows it from Gop Farm (*083 799*) through Newmarket and along its N.E. side as far as *108 787*. It crosses the road at *126 774* and at *132 767*, and uses the Brynbella and Holywell Racecourse mounds (above) for changes of alignment. After a short stretch along the road to *152 752* it is lost until Treuddyn in Area 12.

Maen Achwyfan

ECMW No. 190   *129 787* FL

A richly decorated disc-headed cross of the late X–XI century which has suffered from exposure in its original wayside position. It is an interesting outlier of the Northumbrian type of cross, in that Scandinavian elements in its linear design have been softened by Celtic influence. In State care, accessible at any time without charge.

Moel Arthur
PRRF p. 267   *145 660* FL

Crossing the Clwydian range to the S.W., the mountain road skirts a steep-sided hillfort of 2 ha, defenced by two banks and ditches and a counterscarp bank. The narrow inturned entrance on the N.E. and the simple contour plan suggest an early date. **Penycloddiau** (*128 676*), though less easy to reach, is outstandingly large at 20 ha, but shares the

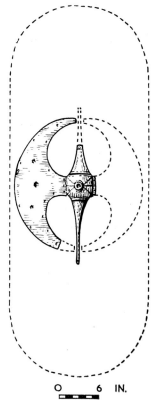

O   6   IN.

Figure 10. Moel Hiraddug (Area 11): the bronze mountings of a shield, probably lost in battle in the final phase of the pre-Roman Iron Age. *After W. J. Hemp.*

simplicity of plan. The N. end has four banks for strength across the
level ridge, and two entrances at the S.E. and N.E.

Moel Hiraddug
Fig. 10; *PRRF* p. 96   *063 785* FL

As at Dinorben (Area 9), quarrying is steadily destroying the defences
of a complex Iron Age fort, but rescue excavations are building up a
picture of its history. The earliest fort, bivallate on the E., was of contour type where the ground allowed. The final scheme of defence made
greater use of strong natural slopes. A hoard of decorative metalwork
found between the defences is dated by its style to the last half-century
before the Romans, though it may have predated the latest fort.

THE LOWER DEE   100 km (62 miles)
AREA 12   Denbighshire DE, Flintshire FL
Map 117; 1″ 108, 109, 118; 2½″ SJ *15, 16, 24–26, 34–36, 45, 46*

The Dee here forms the boundary of modern Wales, as it meanders
along the edge of the Cheshire plain. The transition to higher ground
on the W. is historically of great significance, to which two early medieval dykes bear witness; they are conveniently close together for
comparison in their surviving sections, but for earlier periods the record
is chiefly of chance discoveries and sites no longer open to view. Wrexham, though primarily concerned with the needs of industrial N.E.
Wales, is centrally placed for the limited archaeological tour of the area,
but Chester is a good alternative, providing a suitable start or finish with
its own antiquities and museum.

   The absence of megalithic tombs may well be explained, as in Area
11, by the use of caves for burial by the neolithic population. A series of
excavations near Llandegla by that indefatigable professor, Boyd
Dawkins, from 1869 to 1872 produced the crouched burials of five
individuals in a rockshelter and 16 in a cave at *Perthi Chwarae (188 536)*;
similar cave-burials at *Rhos Ddigre (187 533)* were accompanied by
coarse pottery, flints and a polished stone axe, which gives at least the
probability of a neolithic date for the whole group.

   A change towards the single-burial tradition of the Bronze Age is
seen in the stone cist found at *Brymbo (294 541)*, now transferred entire
with its crouched skeleton and beaker to the National Museum.

Plate 10. A wooden bowl of the Bronze Age from Caergwrle (Area 12), with rich carving and overlay of sheet gold. Full size. *Photo: National Museum of Wales.*

Two surviving cairns low in the valley of the Alun at **Rhual-isaf** (*225 649*) and **Pentrehobin** (*247 625*) give some idea of the situation of the one which once stood at *Mold* (*244 639*), in which was found a skeleton with several hundred amber beads and the gold cape which long masqueraded in the British Museum as a pony's breastplate. Contemporary accounts of the harsh treatment given to this priceless object by its finders make sad reading indeed (*PRRF* p. 256). When a similar cairn at *Llong* (*263 625*) was fully excavated in 1956, a crouched inhumation burial was found lying on a stone platform over a clay-filled pit, and covered by an inner cairn. Grave goods included a jet necklace and many ring beads, confirming the presence in this valley of Middle Bronze Age people whose comparative wealth must have derived from participation in the metal trade of the north Wales coastal route.

Another notable Bronze Age find in the same valley at *Caergwrle* (*311 570*) was a little oval wooden bowl (Plate 10), intricately carved and adorned with finely incised sheet gold. The decoration, arranged schematically to suggest a ship, includes wavy lines round the base for water, vertical lines on the sides for oars, and discs around the rim for shields, while two protective 'eyes' guard the bow, and two the stern.

Moel y Gaer
PRRF p. 57   *211 690* FL

An accessible outlier of the simple contour-type hillforts of the Clwyd-ian hills (see Areas 10, 11), with its entrance on the S.E. through a defence doubled only on the E. where level ground demanded it. A contrasting situation was chosen for the **Bryn Alun** fort, on a narrow ridge in a river bend near Wrexham (*331 537*) where the river itself served for defence on the W., as it served in lieu of Wat's Dyke a thousand years later.

The Grosvenor Museum, Chester
See map, Fig. 12   *404 659*

Although the Wrexham area offers no extant Roman remains, a visit to Chester is strongly recommended. This history of north Wales in that period is inseparable from the affairs of the Twentieth Legion, which controlled the system of roads and forts from the fortress of Deva at Chester, to which part of the museum display forms an admirable guide. The works depot of the legion at *Holt* (*404 546*) has also provided important detail of the administrative affairs of the Roman occupation. The tile and pottery kilns and residential buildings there were fully excavated from 1907 to 1915 (*RFW* p. 42). Another important Roman industrial site at *Ffrith* (*285 552*) was concerned with lead working,

though evidence of actual mining in the lead-bearing hills nearby has
proved elusive.

Wat's Dyke

See map, Fig. 12; *OD* p. 225   *233 697* etc. FL, DE

Built by one of Offa's forebears during the years of Mercian expansion
in the early VIII century A.D., this is the more easterly version of a
frontier laid out to guard the plain from hostile inroads. It makes skilful
use of impassable stretches of the River Alun N. of Wrexham, and of the
Dee near Chirk, to make a continuous barrier from the Dee estuary to
the Severn valley. Surviving sections of the earthwork have an average
width of 14.6 m and a height of 3 m from crest of bank to bottom of
ditch, the latter being on the W. Since a westward-facing slope was
chosen whenever possible, the ditch often becomes a mere shelf, and
material might be obtained from the E. side when occasion demanded.

After an incomplete start near Holywell, the first continuous stretch
can be followed from *233 697* over A55 to *239 674*, after which it is
either hidden or fragmentary until a good section near Buckley (*258
646*) is reached. After several km in varying condition (good at *308 591*)
it is absent for 5 km. The course was straight through Wrexham
between fragments extant at *333 525* and *326 494*. The most continuous
sector can be followed on foot from *323 476* for 5 km till it dwindles
through Wynnstay Park, to resume in Shropshire.

Offa's Dyke

See map, Fig. 12; *OD* p. 29   *267 577* etc. FL, DE

Built at the command of Offa himself in the late VIII century, replacing
Wat's Dyke as the northern part of the total frontier between Mercia
and Wales. Its more westerly line here would, if it had been completed,
give full protection to the S. shore of the Dee estuary; but the incentive
seems to have dwindled, perhaps in the uncertainty of Offa's last years.
After a gap of several km from Holywell Racecourse in Area 11, the
dyke resumes at Treuddyn (*267 577*), being used as the course of the
B5101 to *287 548*, where excavation proved the existence of a ditch on
the W. Cuttings at Ffrith revealed a marking-out post, and proved the
dyke's post-Roman date. Its course over Brymbo Hill is interrupted by
modern development, after crossing B5102 at *288 546*; 2 km from
291 525 are fairly continuously followed by modern lanes. A fine sector
1 km long is accessible at *297 493* and *298 487*; the mound at **Cadwgan
Hall** is unlike a prehistoric barrow or a medieval castle mound, but it
could be a Saxon burial place if there is any substance to the report of

'armour' found in 1804. The last traces before the Dee is negotiated include a fine stretch from *297 441* across A539 and beyond, after leaving **Pen y Gardden** on the W. at *297 448*. This weak contour fort of prehistoric date was clearly not considered to be dangerous as a strong point on the Welsh side of the frontier. In its general characteristics Offa's Dyke is similar to Wat's but is 3 m wider on average, and correspondingly higher.

3 NORTH CENTRAL RIVERS
The Dee and Severn

Figure 11. Gaer Fawr (Area 16): a bronze boar, possibly of Roman date, supposed to have been found in the hillfort. Full size. *After E. L. Barnwell.*

THE MIDDLE DEE   95 km (59 miles)
AREA 13   Denbighshire DE, Merioneth ME
   Map 116, 117, 125, 126; 1″ 108, 109, 117, 118; 2½″ SJ *13, 14, 23, 24*

The event of the year at Llangollen is the International Eisteddfod, the July festival at which the Welsh play host to the traditional singers and dancers of the world. The out-of-season visitor is equally welcome, and could use this base with advantage for the neighbouring Areas 10, 12, 14, and 15 as well. There is a small local museum in **Plas Newydd**.

The great depth to which the Dee and its tributaries have cut into the eastern edge of the Welsh mountains has not materially affected the uniformity of the landscape. These are wild moorlands above 300 m, bearing little more than Bronze Age cairns; on the N. is a broad expanse which is accessible from mountain roads, while on the S. the ridge rises westward to the remote heights of the Berwyns and the backbone of Wales. The valleys and the lower hillslopes were colonised by Celtic farmers whose tribal cohesion through Roman times must have contributed to the strength that determined the course of Offa's Dyke as the Mercian frontier in the VIII century A.D.

Hendom
HM p. 77   *136 430* ME
Standing close to the A5 road, this artificial mound is probably sepulchral in spite of its similarity to many medieval castle mounds, like Owain Glyndwr's Mount 1 km up the valley. Within the kerb of stones seen on the N. there is a height of 6 m of built-up gravel.

A circuit to the N. leads to a group of less impressive cairns; at **Pantymaen** (*158 478*) the stone standing on the damaged mound, to a total height of 3 m, is an unusual feature, but the three mounds at **Ty-mawr** (*161 482*) are rather more typical of upland valleys at 30 m diameter and 1 m high. From here a walk of 3 km over Llantysilio Mountain to the Horseshoe Pass would take in **Moel y Gamelin** (*176 465*), a fine mountain-top cairn.

On the next summit to the west is yet another hillfort called **Moel y Gaer** (*167 463*), but here a small single-ramparted oval with two possible entrances, unlike the larger Clwydian forts of Area 10.

Eliseg's Pillar and Cairn
ECMW No. 182   *202 445* DE

The most famous memorial in Wales, set up here on a low mound and inscribed with a fulsome panegyric of the princely house of Powys, has suffered greatly from Civil War vandalism and more than a thousand years of weathering, so that it can no longer be read. Only a careful transcript by Edward Lhuyd in 1696 has revealed it to be a IX century tribute by Cyngen, who died in A.D. 854, to his great-grandfather Elise, the contemporary and chief opponent of Offa of Mercia. The lower part of the shaft and the cross-head are missing.

The mound, on which the remaining portion of the shaft was reset in 1779, was opened and found to contain an inhumation in a stone chamber, with a silver coin. The skull was reburied after gilding, an extravagance fitting for an ancestor of the Powys line—for this is thought to be a sub-Roman chieftain's tomb of the V or VI century, chosen as a site for the pillar because of its royal association. The pillar is in State care, always accessible without charge. A pamphlet is available.

Dinas Bran
PRRD p. 252   *223 430* DE

While the most obvious remains are those of the medieval castle, the earliest structure here was a fair-sized hillfort. The single line of defence can be easily followed in the open round the E. shoulder of the hill, but the entrance works at the S.W. could not be disentangled from those of the castle without excavation.

Creigiau Eglwyseg Cairns
PRRD p. 257 etc.   *223 442* etc. DE

The moorland to the N.E. of Llangollen ends abruptly on its W. side in a cliff 5 km long, above which the shoulder of the hill is lined with a variety of Bronze Age monuments. They are better visited in a single walk than individually from the road which follows the foot of the scree

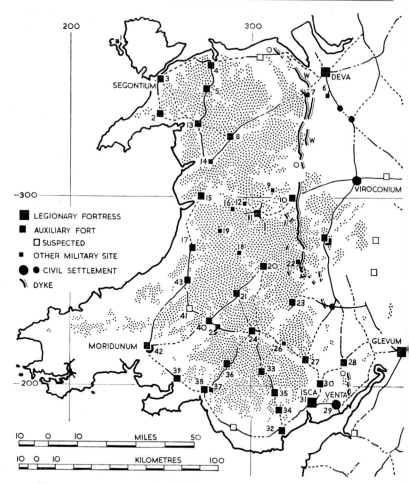

Figure 12. Roman control of Wales with a system of roads and forts—and Mercian control of the frontier in the VII century. *After V. E. Nash-Williams, M. G. Jarrett et al.*

1, Caer Gybi (Area 1). 2, Pen Llystyn (A4). 3, Segontium (A5). 4, Caerhun (A7). 5, Bryn y Gefeiliau (A8). 6, Holt (A12). 7, Ffrith (A12). 8, Caer Gai (A14). 9, Gibbet Hill (A15). 10, Forden Gaer (A16). 11, Caersws (A17). 12, Caer Noddfa (A17). 13, Tomen y Mur (A18). 14, Brithdir (A20). 15, Pennal (A21). 16, Pen y Crogbren (A21). 17, Trawscoed (A22). 18, Esgairperfedd (A23). 19, Cae Gaer (A23). 20, Castell Collen (A24). 21, Caerau (A24). 22, Discoed (A25). 23, Clyro (A26). 24, Brecon Gaer (A27). 25, Y Pigwn (A27). 26, Pen y Gaer (A28). 27, Abergavenny (A28). 28, Monmouth (A28). 29,

slope 200 m below. The sites are: *223 442*, cairn with two cists; *224 444*, cairn 8 m in diameter; *222 449*, cairn 21 m in diameter, 2 m high; two smaller cairns nearby; *223 449*, earth circle 10 m in diameter, bank 1.5 m wide; *224 455*, first of a series of four cairns, the last being 1.5 km to the N.; *227 449*, standing stone, 2 m high, leaning; *228 451*, cairn circle of 40 stones, 16 m in diameter; *229 452*, *233 459*, *231 463*, three cairns 1 m high, last two on ridge. Further up the mountain road on **Cefn y Gader** are several good cairns. One near the road at *238 497* is 24 m in diameter and 2.5 m high.

Offa's Dyke
Fig. 12; *OD* p. 54   *281 406* etc. DE
From just beyond Froncysyllte the Dyke can be picked up as it leaves the Dee, and followed across the Ceiriog valley to where it leaves modern Wales at *251 335*. It is generally well preserved over this whole stretch, though much of it is in private parkland. Good viewpoints are at *281 406*, *271 391*, *263 374* and at three lane crossings before it climbs Selattyn Hill from the B4579 at *252 349*. In the last stretch the ditch is disproportionately small, since much of the bank material was taken from the uphill side.

The Ceiriog valley road leads to Llanarmon, near which **Cerrig Gwynion** hillfort (*152 340*) is a fair example of a univallate site, with traces of huts averaging 9 m in diameter on the south-facing slope within. The marginal land of this valley has several sizeable summit cairns, of which **Tomen y Meirw** (*162 381*) is the most accessible on the return journey to Llangollen.

THE UPPER DEE   104 km (65 miles)
AREA   14   Denbighshire DE, Merioneth ME
Map 116, 125; 1″ 108, 116, 117; 2½″ SH *82, 83, 93, 94*, SJ *03, 04*

Tourist development is gaining ground at Bala, which lies at the end of

Caerwent (A29). 30, Usk (A30). 31, Caerleon (A30). 32, Cardiff (A31). 33, Merthyr Tydfil (A33). 34, Caerphilly (A33). 35, Gelligaer (A33). 36, Coelbren (A34). 37, Blaen-cwm-bach (A34). 38, Neath (A34). 39, Loughor (A34). 40, Llandovery (A36). 41, Dolaucothi (A36). 42, Carmarthen (A37). 43, Llanio (A38). O, Offa's Dyke (A11, 12, 13, 16, 25). W, Wat's Dyke (A11, 12).

the great Llyn Tegid in a key position, and is the meeting point of several mountain and valley routes. It is the heart of the 'heartland' of Wales, and will certainly provide all the Welsh atmosphere that the visitor could want.

The mountain core of north-central Wales is generally bare of pre-historic remains, apart from isolated Bronze Age cairns, and even now only reservoirs, mountain roads and forestry plantations have left their mark. Though the high ground doubtless provided valuable pasturage, it is only along valleys like the Upper Dee that the archaeological sequence can be traced. Here was fertile ground for Iron Age farmers, and the Roman military system made good use of the natural passage from east to west. (Fig. 12.)

Caer Gai
RFW p. 54; *HM* p. 235   *877 315* ME
The choice of site for this Roman fort is typically effective, on a low but dominant spur in a broad valley. The S.W. and S.E. sides are well preserved as seen from the outside, but the interior has been filled level, and the N. corner obscured by farm development. The entrance gap in the S.W. side is clearly seen; outside the N.E. gate was a wayside shrine to Hercules, from which an inscription survives to tell of the presence of the First Cohort of Nervii, auxiliary cavalry from northern Gaul who were in Britain in the II century A.D. Excavations have con-firmed military occupation up to *c*. A.D. 130, without any rebuilding of the barracks in stone.

Moel Caws Hut Group
HM p. 205   *845 274* ME
An easy walk of 1 km leads to the only well-preserved Iron Age settle-ment of the area, apart from hillforts. It consists of three enclosures on the bank of a stream at the lower end of a broad upland valley. The W. one contains two deeply terraced huts 10 m in diameter; another in the E. enclosure has been obscured by incorporation in a medieval house platform. The third enclosure below has one smaller hut.

Caer Euni
Pl. 11; *HM* p. 137   *000 412* ME
Sited high on a narrow ridge, the system of rampart, ditch and counter-scarp bank is an enlargement of an earlier fort, of which the obsolete cross-bank can be traced in the interior, along with the sites of some 25 round huts. The fused stone to be seen at the W. corner probably has no

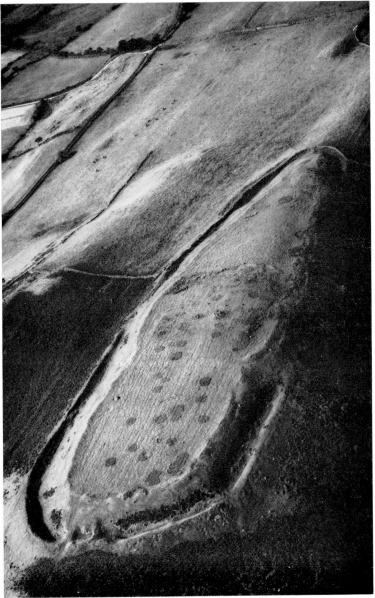

Plate 11. Caer Euni (Area 14): a two-period Iron Age fort. *Photo: J. K. S. St. Joseph.*

connection with the vitrified forts of Scotland. Two **cairn circles** at *993 410* are within reach on this ridge.

Caer Caradog
PRRD p. 234   *968 479* DE

Excavations at this univallate fort have shown that a ditchless bank was followed in a second period by a larger one associated with a rock-cut ditch, but no trace of timber work nor dating evidence was found. The entrance was only half as wide as it now appears.

Caer Drewin
HM p. 144   *088 444* ME

The latest interpretation of this complicated site invokes four periods of construction. At first a small hilltop earthwork curved in a U shape to end against a steep natural scarp on the N. Only the E. half of this remains, with its original entrance, as an annexe to the surviving fort, of which the stone rampart on the crest of the hill, with a deeply inturned entrance way, compares closely in style with Tre'r Ceiri and other sites of Lleyn (Area 3). Revetment can be clearly seen in places, with a slight batter outside, but no ditch, and a rampart walk within. The W. half of the stone fort has its own smaller entrance and is of slighter build, its material being supposedly derived from an earlier enclosure which would have served for protection of cattle rather than as a tribal refuge. Two round huts finally enclosed in the V-shaped annexe are contemporary or later dwellings, and can be compared with the small oblong fort of **Moel Fodig** (*096 456*), which also has traces of two huts inside, and was presumably a homestead of family size from the outset. A Roman date for such sites would repeat the history of settlement in the North-west (Areas 2, 5).

The broad valley bottom of the Dee between Bala and Corwen contains several round cairns showing a variety of constructional features. At *Rug* (*056 439*) the medieval castle mound conceals an original Bronze Age barrow, with a central cist that has been preserved in a recent chamber. A low barrow at **Gwerclas** (*054 421*) has a kerb of large stones on one side, while at **Tyfos-uchaf** (*028 388*) a more complete circle of thirteen stones remains after the removal of most of the large mound. A centrally placed cist at **Branas-uchaf** (*011 375*) is poorly preserved, but must have been of megalithic proportions.

The mountains have their share of cairns, but to visit them involves many miles on foot (see Area 15). However, a cairn circle on **Moel Ty-uchaf** (*056 371*) is reasonably accessible from the valley, and is

notable for its completeness. Forty-one contiguous stones up to 1 m
high make up the kerb, of which the outer face forms a circle 12 m in
diameter, with a gap of 3 m on the S.E. The central hollow results from
robbing of a burial cist, but there was probably no covering mound.

THE VYRNWY	122 km (76 miles)
AREA 15	Denbighshire DE, Montgomeryshire MY
	Map 125, 136; 1″ 117; 2½″ SH 90–92, SJ 00–03, 10–13

To the urban north-west of England Llyn Vyrnwy has meant a good
water supply since 1891, and there is plenty of it coming down the face of
the Berwyn range. The lake lies in a densely forested area, and controls
the headwaters of the Vyrnwy river itself, but the Twrch, Banwy and
Tanat flow freely in lush valleys cut deep into the mountains, all of them
joining the Severn near the English border. Llanfyllin, an ancient
borough of Powys and an agricultural centre today, is central to the
area, but other quiet villages also offer accommodation. Oswestry and
Welshpool are the nearest towns giving more choice.

This is essentially motoring country in which the archaeological sites
are often secluded in farmland and woods, or remote on the mountains.
On the lower ridges are fortified sites of varying size and complexity,
the settlements and refuges of a well-established tribal population.
Some no doubt originated in the early days of the Kingdom of Powys,
continuing native traditions that were little changed by the Roman
interlude, so the obviously multi-period sites may well have been continuously occupied from Iron Age times to the Norman conquest.
Isolated stretches of boundary dyke also testify to a strong territorial
possessiveness.

The A490 road across the wooded ridge east of Llanfyllin passes
close to the strong hillfort in **Bryngwyn Wood** (*183 178*). The bank and
ditch along the north side and round the ends did not need to be continued on the precipitous south side. A separate wall and ditch inside
must belong to a second phase. The winding descent into the Vyrnwy
valley then passes the northern end of **Bwlch y Cibau Dyke** (*186 172*
to *181 166*), 1 km long in an L shape that guards the broad hilltop. An
overall height of 3 m and breadth of 10 m is best seen in the northern
arm. On a spur beyond the Vyrnwy is **Cefn Du Camp** (*150 094*),

Plate 12. Mathrafal (Area 15): a Dark Age stronghold. The castle mound is a Norman addition. *Photo: R.C.A.M., Crown Copyright.*

another wooded hillfort, simple in shape but strongly fortified, the double line of defence becoming triple at the N.E. end where the entrance lies.

Mathrafal Castle

Pl. 12; *INV* No. 583   *132 108* MY

In a slightly elevated position where the Banwy joins the Vyrnwy, and with a view down the valley beyond Meifod, this is one of the more tantalising sites in Wales, for the name appears in early Welsh literature as the stronghold of princes, even though there is no firm basis for the tradition that this was the direct successor to Pengwern (Shrewsbury) when the capital there fell to Offa of Mercia in the VIII century A.D. These are the events which would truly bring the Dark Ages of archaeology to life if their exact locations could be identified. The rampart of earth and stone encloses an area about 100 m square, the accompanying ditch being most pronounced on the S., where it is overlooked from higher ground. This weakness in defence denies the alternative of a Roman origin; later the enclosure was used as the bailey of a XIII century motte placed in the N.E. angle.

Gibbet Hill Roman Fortlet
Fig. 12; *RFW* p. 142   *106 044* MY

The Roman occupation of Wales did not leave a very distinct impression on the terrain which lay at the limits of both the Chester and Caerleon commands, but communications between the two would not have been neglected. The small rectangular fortification here, 50 m by 46 m, had a turf-faced rampart with an entrance in the east side, and was possibly intended as a signal station of the initial conquest, but it was never finished.

Llys y Cawr   *064 133* MY

Regaining the Vyrnwy valley by the B4382, the route towards the Berwyns bends northwards around the steep-sided hill of Allt Dolanog, on which stands the so-called 'Giant's Court'. Its two banks average 2 to 3.5 m in height, best seen where they face more level ground on the N.

Craig Rhiwarth Hillfort
Fig. 13; *PEW* p. 138   *057 270* MY

The number of stone hut foundations on the hilltop here has never

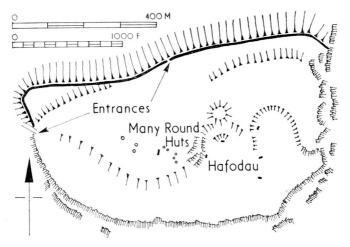

Figure 13. Craig Rhiwarth (Area 15): sketch plan of the main features of the fort. *After A. H. A. Hogg.*

been accurately recorded, let alone surveyed. Many original round huts show signs of reconstruction, suggesting a long history of occupation from Iron Age times, ending with a few rectangular *hafodau* of late medieval date. There is a precipitous fall of some 350 m to the south, so that only the N. side needed artificial defence, now seen as a ruinous stone wall above a steep natural scarp, with a simple entrance in the middle, and a slanting one at the W. end. The disheartening results of excavations in 1933 led to the strange conclusion that the remains were an illusion of nature.

Rhosybeddau Circle and Alignment
SCW p. 120   *059 303* MY

Stone alignments are rare enough in Wales to make this compulsory viewing. Sited on a shelf at the meeting of two streams, it bears a marked resemblance to the Cerrig Duon site in Area 34. Two parallel lines of inconspicuous stones, 15 remaining on the N. and 24 on the S. side, are spaced at roughly 3 m intervals and lead W. towards the circle, with which they were probably never actually connected; nor indeed do the two features have a common central alignment. The circle is deficient on the W. side, but the nine low stones on the E. show it to have been about 12.2 m in diameter.

On the same northern side of the **Afon Disgynfa** at *071 297* is a simple burial cairn 15 m across and 1 m high. Only in the broadest sense can it be said to be of the same age as the last site, for when comparing Bronze Age monuments it is rarely that excavation has provided the evidence for dating even to the nearest century. The cairns of the high Berwyn ridge, starting at *Moel Sych* (*066 318*) and ending 3 km to the N.N.E. at *Cadair Bronwen* (*077 347*), are interesting for their constructional variety, but the rest is guesswork, even the mild suggestion that their occupants must have belonged to an elevated social class to merit such prominent graves.

One careful excavation of a burial monument in this district can be thankfully recorded. At *Ysgwennant* (*189 305*) an oval mound measuring 41 m by 23 m produced portions of two beakers, one being in a pit with jet buttons and rings and a flint knife, as well as charcoal which gave a radiocarbon date around 1500 B.C.—a result which is inexplicably three centuries younger than might be expected on conventional chronology. While this sort of discrepancy may in due course be resolved, a genuine scepticism must be applied to the recorded finding, a century ago, of a 'brass kettle, armour and coins' in *Carnedd Illog* (*051 239*).

Maes Mochnant Stone
PRRD p. 303   *137 248* DE

This pillar can be declared prehistoric, and a probable Bronze Age burial marker, without considering any later alternatives. It was carefully chosen for its rectangular section, which diminishes upwards from 1.1 m by 0.4 m near the base to its full height of 3.5 m. It can be seen from the road, but approach from the farm on the east is possible. Another stone, about 3 m high, which stands by the roadside in **Llanrhaedr Village** (*125 259*), was used since 1770 as a milestone and as a lamp post, as its Latin inscriptions tell. It once stood on a mound nearby, and even that was not its original site, so that its prehistoric origin cannot be more than a possibility.

Llwyn Bryn Dinas
INV No. 489   *172 247* DE

Sited on a prominent hill bordering the road along the N. side of the Tanat valley, this hillfort of about 3 ha exemplifies a typologically early fortification, with its single rampart following the contours and a simple inturned entrance on the S.E., the whole unaltered by later work.

Tynewydd and Abernaint Dykes
INV Nos. 634 & 635   *133 232* & *125 218* MY

Both are well preserved and easily accessible, and both face northward as though belonging to the same strategic concept, though the second is unusual in facing uphill. Both would have served to impede progress from the Tanat valley into the Llanfyllin area, and may be of comparatively late medieval origin.

THE MIDDLE SEVERN   53 km (33 miles)
AREA 16   Montgomeryshire MY
Map 125, 126, 136, 137; 1″ 117, 118, 128; 2½″ SJ *10, 20–22, 31*, SO *28, 29*

Just before its emergence from Wales the Severn passes along a broad valley between two strong ridges of hills, the Long Mountain on the east with Montgomery at its S. end, and a more broken series of hills on the west with Welshpool in a strategic gap near the middle. Just as the castles of these two towns have dominated the scene in historic times, so for prehistory it is the fortified hilltops that are of greatest significance here. There is good evidence too of the way the Romans, and in turn the powerful Mercians of the VIII century, imposed their own particular strategy on the valley. A visit to *Shrewsbury* town and **Museum** will help to complete the picture from the English side.

Welshpool and Montgomery provide accommodation, but wayside guest houses are frequent in an area that sees a great flow of tourist traffic in summer.

The Powysland Museum, Welshpool   *226 077* MY

This museum, which is affiliated to the National Museum of Wales, houses the collections of the Powysland Club, founded in 1867 and thus one of the oldest antiquarian societies in Wales. Apart from casual finds from the county, including important groups of Bronze Age and Roman bronzes, there are fragments of the shield and decorated plaques from Moel Hiraddug (Area 11), and pottery from Forden Gaer (below). Hours of opening are variable, since there is no full-time curator, but 14.00–16.30 is standard, Weds. & Suns. excepted, with a further hour on summer evenings.

The hillforts in the northward loop of this tour from Welshpool are for those who enjoy climbing and pathfinding. **Gaer Fawr** (*224 130*), not far from a lane but well wooded, has triple defences on the N.W., representing a complex history similar to that of Ffridd Faldwyn (see below), and an entrance in each end of its 300 m length. The miniature bronze boar (Fig. 11) found here is unlikely to indicate a Roman phase, even though the boar was the badge of the Twentieth Legion stationed at Chester. **Llanymynech Hill** (*265 220*) in contrast is open ground (partly a golf course), but has been so extensively quarried and mined since Roman times that prehistoric features are hard to distinguish. A notable exception is where the rampart near the western edge was used as part of **Offa's Dyke**, which can be seen again south of Llanymynech where it crosses roads at *273 174* and *275 164*.

Cefn y Castell
INV No. 796   *305 134* MY
The long, narrow summit of Middletown Hill, the north-eastern summit of the companion ridge to Breiddin Hill, is almost entirely occupied by a multivallate fort of classic form. The substantial rampart has been built of material from outside, leaving a noticeable shelf, and from quarry hollows inside. Of the two entrances in the ends, the N.E.

one is especially noteworthy for its long, inturned passageway. There is a slight, outer line of defence further down the slope, but it was not carried all round the hill. **Bausley Hill Camp** (*321 145*) on the lower, N.E. end of the ridge has a simpler entrance, and the defences are multiple, except on the S.E. side.

The Breiddin
PEW p. 135   *292 144* MY

The hillfort here is better sited than its two neighbours, having both a more naturally defensible perimeter and a greater internal area. The central entrance through artificial defences on the gentler S.E. side also faces **New Pieces**, where extramural agriculture has left its mark in square-shaped 'celtic fields' and what may have been a defensible cattle enclosure. The main rampart, running from a crevice at the N.E. corner to the W. cliff, and an outer line of lesser extent, are of stone with no apparent ditch, but a ditched defence was added N.E. of the slanting entrance passage. Excavation in advance of the usual threat of quarrying has also revealed an earlier phase of timber-faced defence, and in general supports the sequence suggested by the excavations of 1933–5. After an initial, probably undefended, Late Bronze Age occupation, a settlement of timber round huts was lightly defended in the I century A.D., then strongly fortified in stone against the Romans. Though probably not fully refortified after the conquest, the hilltop was extensively reoccupied in the IV century for perhaps more than 300 years.

Offa's Dyke
Fig. 12; *OD* p. 89   *249 077* etc. MY

The strategy of the placing of the dyke along the E. side of the Severn, near the foot of the Long Mountain rather than on its heights, has been lucidly explained by the late Sir Cyril Fox in his published field study. This was a frontier established by treaty rather than a defence, and as such would pass west of land already in Mercian control, though always maintaining a commanding view to the Welsh side. Opposite Welshpool, however, the dyke swings up to the 250 m level in a way that suggests concession of some better land to the demands of Powys. The dyke can be seen at several points on roads, but best at *249 077*, *243 026* and *238 020*, then parallel to the road to Forden. Past Montgomery the dyke coincides partly with the present-day border, the best preserved portions being accessible at *235 975* and *245 947*. A purpose strategically connected with the dyke is suggested for **Caer Din** (*273 897*) on the grounds of its rectilinear shape.

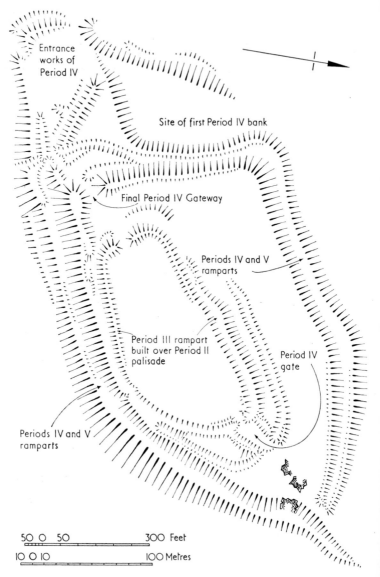

Figure 14. Ffridd Faldwyn (Area 16): the development of the hillfort. *After B. H. St. J. O'Neil.*

The course of the *Roman road* from Wroxeter (Viroconium) into mid-Wales (Fig. 12) does not pass along Long Mountain from Westbury as on the O.S. 1 inch map, but has now been identified following a more typical Roman route which enters Wales at *262 011*, where its *agger* can be seen in a bend of the modern road. Its destination was the auxiliary fort probably to be identified as Lavobrinta, but known today as *Forden Gaer (208 989)*. Though not easily seen in the cultivated fields, this has been reasonably assessed, with the help of minor excavations, as a cavalry fort measuring 186 m by 167 m, just over 3 ha in area.

Ffridd Faldwyn
PEW p. 140   *217 969* MY
The prominent spur looking down on Montgomery's medieval castle and town from the west was occupied in the Neolithic period, but its first defence was a double palisade in the III century B.C. enclosing 1.2 ha at the summit. (See Fig. 14, Period II.) Excavation in 1937–9, cut short by war, revealed a complex sequence of perhaps as many as four more Iron Age fortifications. The palisade was succeeded by a timber-laced rampart with two widely spaced ditches and bridged gateway, all thoroughly reduced to a vitrified state by fire. The Period IV replacement of the early I century B.C. was on a far more ambitious scale, the stone-faced bank with a ditch 6 m wide enclosing fully 4 ha. The surviving rampart at the entrance represents a revision of this fort, lessening it to 3.2 ha along with renewal of the ditch of the original inner fort. Finally, hurried repairs to the whole fort (Period V) must be ascribed to the threat of the Roman advance in *c.* A.D. 50, which put an end to the use of the hilltop as a tribal refuge.

Pen-y-foel
INV No. 92   *178 059* MY
A fine hillfort with an annexe, of about 2 ha total area, on the end of a small craggy ridge. Artificial defences are hard to detect on three sides, but a strong bank and ditch protect the W. end of the main enclosure. Here was one of the two possible entrances, through the annexe, the other being where the present track rises to the top of the S.s carp.

THE UPPER SEVERN   55 km (34 miles)
AREA 17   Montgomeryshire MY
            Map 136; 1″ 128; 2½″ SN *98, 99*, SO *08, 09, 18, 19*

Llanidloes and Newtown are old market towns which flourished on the
wool trade, and have now turned to an interest in tourism, for which
they are strategically placed on routes that are both east–west and north–
south at the same time—a position fully appreciated by the Romans in
the siting of Caersws as a pivot of the military road system.

The Severn already has the makings of a great river in its upper
reaches, where it is joined by several tributaries which have an almost
equal claim to the name. The flood water is now partly controlled by the
Clywedog reservoir in the eastern foothills of Plynlimon, between steep-
sided ridges that carry a group of hillforts now made more accessible.
The Bronze Age barrows of the area are harder to reach, but their
presence tells of the nomadic shepherds who went before the fort-
dwellers. From this early time the Kerry Ridgeway afforded contact to
the E. and several fine barrows are sited near the cross-ridge dykes which,
in early medieval times, barred that same freedom of movement.

The dykes of the Kerry ridge, considered as a group (Fig. 12),
probably represent the piecemeal assertion of territorial rights before
the great frontier work of Offa's Dyke imposed political formality in the
late VIII century. Their present appearance as chains of isolated
fragments is not due to the passage of time so much as to their original
purpose, which was to supplement natural features such as streams and
marshes. **The Wantyn Dyke** can be seen at road crossings at *191 907*
and *185 919*, but its higher sections are harder to reach. The **Double
Dyche** is similarly disjointed, but the siting of its sections at *103 857*,
116 850 and *120 843* is easy to comprehend.

Cefn Carnedd
INV No. 334   *017 900* MY
The stiff climb leads to what is undoubtedly one of the most interesting
hillforts of mid-Wales, potentially a key site for Iron Age history if
fully excavated. The triple defences cover some 6 ha and must represent
several phases, including an earlier, smaller fort of only 1.6 ha at the
S.W. end. The final phase, a small area cut off by a straight bank, may
even be of Romano-British date, if the nearness of the Caersws fort
does not preclude this.

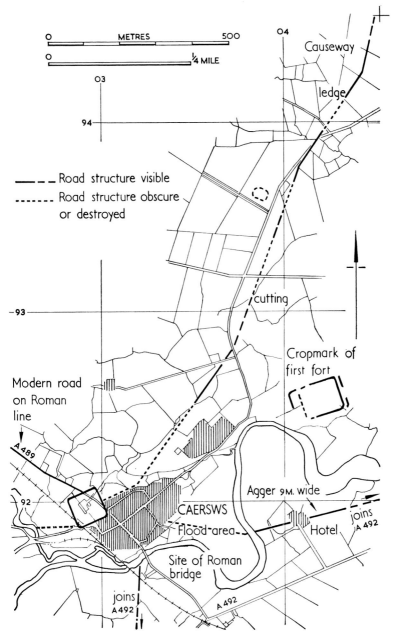

METRES 500

¼ MILE

O3

94

04

Causeway

ledge

━ ━ ━ Road structure visible
••••••• Road structure obscure
or destroyed

cutting

-93

Cropmark of
first fort

Modern road
on Roman
line

A 489

92

CAERSWS

Flood area

Agger 9m. wide

Hotel

joins
A 492

Site of Roman
bridge

joins
A 492

A 492

Figure 15. Caersws (Area 17): Roman roads and forts at an important control point. *After G. D. B. Jones.*

Pen y Clun
INV No. 595   *926 875* MY
Though small (0.6 ha), and only sited on the lower end of Bryn-y-tail,
the position has natural strength on three sides. No artificial work was
needed on the E., and on the N. and S. only a single bank, increasing
towards the entrance at the W., where a strong ditch is added on the
outside. About 35 m down towards the saddle are vestiges of a further
line of defence.

Of the hilltops nearby, *Penycastell* (*946 881*) has widely spaced double
ramparts, now mainly destroyed, *Dinas* (*906 891*) provides an example of
unfinished fortification, curiously sited below its summit, while the
camp marked on the 1 inch map on *Fan Hill* (*931 884*) must be
mentioned, if only to point out that it is imaginary.

Pen-y-gaer
INV No. 593   *908 869* MY
This fortified summit is newly accessible from the reservoir circuit road,
a simple 0.3 ha, but of interest for its stone construction without ditch.
The outer face is easily found in places, and the gateway is clearly
defined where it passes obliquely between overlapping wall ends on the
S.

Caersws Roman Fort
Figs. 12, 15; *RFW* p. 66   *029 920* MY
The earliest fort at this natural focus of communications was discovered
from the air in 1958, and probably functioned only during the original
penetration of mid-Wales in the middle of the I century A.D. It was
about 3.8 ha in area, had three ditches, and was well sited above the
flood level of the Severn. The present village takes its name from the
second fort, which lay at the meeting point of five roads of the military
system established after A.D. 78. This was less well sited—one supposed
outer defence was for protection against flooding of the Afon Carno on
the south—and was only 3.1 ha in area. Its raised platform is easily seen
from the main road passing through it, but the S. corner has been lost to
the railway, and the external bath house lies under the goods shed.
A complicated sequence of structural phases in the defence system has
been revealed by the excavations of 1966–7. An original turf rampart was
slighted into its ditch and rebuilt in the late I century, while the final
fort of the II century had its rampart face and central buildings of
stone, though the barracks were still of timber. Occupation continued

until after A.D. 400, both in the fort and in the civil settlement outside, where pottery is frequently found in village gardens.

The slight trace of *Caer Noddfa* at Carno (*963 966*), though neither rectangular nor proved to be of Roman date, is thought to be a minor fortlet on the route north-westward from Caersws. The roads diverging from Caersws can best be viewed at **Red House** (*052 922*), where the line of the modern road is continued at the bend, and north of **New House** (*046 956*) at a descent from higher ground.

4 THE CAMBRIAN COAST
Merioneth and Plynlimon

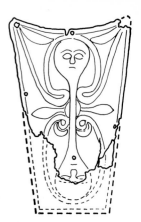

Figure 16. A decorative bronze plaque from a late Celtic shield, part of a hoard of objects found near Tal-y-llyn (Area 21). Scale 1:3. *National Museum of Wales.*

THE DWYRYD
AREA 18

53 km (33 miles)
Merioneth ME
Map 124; 1″ 116; 2½″ SH *52, 53, 63, 73*

The convoluted estuary of the Dwyryd is an impediment to purposeful travel around Cardigan Bay, but the prehistoric record in all periods shows no clear break between the mountain areas to N. and S., because new cultural influences were usually distributed evenly by sea-borne immigrants. A fine selection of sites is concentrated near a short stretch of road high up behind Harlech. To these can be added a sortie into the fringes of the broad moorland around Trawsfynydd, where the nuclear power station by the lake is a modern enterprise which can be viewed with praise or regret according to the progressiveness of one's attitude to such things. Harlech and its neighbouring villages provide the first choice for a base in this area.

Muriau Gwyddelod
HM p. 198   *586 302* ME
Side by side in an extensive area of terraced fields are two Iron Age settlements of contrasting type, though they may have been in use at the same time for different purposes. One consists of three close-set round huts facing inwards to a courtyard, which is completed by short connecting walls; the other is a polygonal yard 12 m across, containing a

single round hut. Both are linked into a larger enclosure which forms
the nucleus of the surrounding fields.

Trackway and Standing Stones
HM pp. 56–64   *583 270* etc. ME
The tall, isolated monoliths that are such a familiar feature in Welsh
archaeology, most commonly under the term *maenhir*, have been shown
in several cases to be burial markers of the Bronze Age (see Areas 5,
43). A strong case exists here for their erection as the markers of an
ancient route across mountainous country, where natural hazards abound.
Such routes would have reached a peak of importance in the later Bronze
Age, when metal trading was at its height among nomadic people living
on the uplands. The first pair, in a succession of 13 stones, are to be
found in **Llanbedr** village (*583 270*), from where the route ascends
directly to the N.; it is followed by the modern lane from a small slab
at *Rhiw-goch* (*595 305*), past the tapering column of **Carreg** (*599 309*),
to the tallest stone 400 m further on (*602 313*); on the right there
follows a succession of five smaller stones, ending near *Moel Goedog* at
609 323. The natural route then swings round the northern end of the
Rhinog range and turns S.E. towards Maen Llwyd and Llech Idris
(see below).

To the left of the trackway at *605 324* is a good specimen of a mas-
sively built single hut, nearly 10 m in diameter, associated with cultivation
terraces above the steep drop to the coast. A poorly preserved hut of
similar size, concentrically placed in an enclosure of 30 m diameter near
Erw Wen (*607 323*), was superimposed on the terrace system, and in
its turn was followed by three rectangular huts in a medieval field
system.

Moel Goedog Circles
HM p. 88   *610 324* ME
Any internal cairns that there may have been have now gone, but the
encircling kerb of one of these two is complete, and double on one side.
It is chiefly the relatively small size (7 m diameter) and the contiguous
arrangement of the stones that distinguish such circles from truly
ritual sites such as the Druids' Circle (Area 7).

Moel Goedog Hut Groups
HM p. 195   *616 322* ME
The two groups here are about 120 m apart, at the back of a fairly level
tract of ground bearing traces of division into fields. Only the western

one is well preserved, consisting of four circular rooms, and one of longer shape set round a yard of massive construction, with an external yard on the south. The robbing of the eastern group may be partly due to the imposition of later huts.

Moel Goedog Hillfort

HM p. 148   *616 325* ME

The twin banks of this almost circular fort could hardly have been an effective defence by themselves, but must be merely the basis of a strong timber structure. Such a palisaded site has been dated by excavation at Castell Odo (Area 3) to the III or IV century B.C. The position at the summit of a continuous rise of 370 m from the coast would have served well as a refuge for the farmers who first occupied this part of the Cardigan Bay periphery, whether or not any of the nearby hut settlements are to be regarded as contemporary. A simple gap on the S.W. is the only feasible site for an entrance, presumably also elaborated in timber.

For those whose appetite for cairn circles and hut settlements is not yet satisfied, there are several more within a 7 km walk by keeping the same N.E. direction starting at **Moel y Glo** (*626 343*), where four round huts near the Afon Eisingrug, joined into a group by enclosure walls, exhibit an orthostatic contruction. Near the stream south of **Y Gyrn**, at *640 359* and *641 359*, are three mutilated cairns, one having a ring bank 2 m wide, another a cist within. There are more unenclosed huts

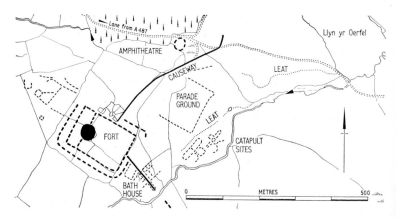

Figure 17. Tomen y Mur (Area 18): the Roman fort and its surroundings. *After R.C.A.M., Crown Copyright.*

in a sheltered recess at *645 349*, and a pair of round huts in an enclosure at *645 352*. 300 m to the N.E. is a cairn in **Bryn Cader Faner** (*648 353*); its burial cist is destroyed, but a distinctive feature is a circle of 15 upright stones about 1 m high, leaning outwards within the body of the mound.

Tomen y Mur
Figs. 12, 17; *RFW* p. 111   *706 386* ME
On the edge of a great expanse of moorland stretching eastward the

Plate 13. A choice specimen of Celtic design from Trawsfynydd (Area 18): the wooden staves of the tankard were found intact in their bronze bindings. Scale 1:2. *Photo: City of Liverpool Museums.*

Romans built this fort as a control post at the start of their western route to the south, an essential component of the strategic structure imposed after the conquest of A.D. 78. The original garrison, probably of cavalry, occupied a fort of 1.7 ha, which was reduced in the early II century to 1.34 ha for perhaps only 20 years of use by an infantry unit. The first fort was of turf and timber, seen in abandoned condition at the N.W. end. The stone-faced rampart of the later fort is best seen on the S.E. side, where the central gateway is reasonably clear, but the Norman motte which is so prominent has obscured the reducing rampart. The internal buildings seem never to have been of stone, though the bath house by the stream on the S.E. was necessarily so. Other external structures which testify to the preparedness of a remote outpost are the levelled parade ground on the N.E., with *ballista* (siege-engine) plat-forms nearby, and the so-called amphitheatre, probably a demonstration arena. Two small enclosures on the N.W. are 'practice camps', the by-product of field exercises, as are the group of five at **Dolddinas** (*734 378*), on the line of the road towards Caer Gai (Area 14).

The Bronze Age trackway which was followed at the start of this tour from Llanbedr continues from here over the mountains eastward, its final markers being *Maen Llwyd* (*707 329*) and **Llech Idris** (*730 310*). The latter is a fine, pointed slab 3.2 m high and 1.4 m wide.

THE RHINOGS WEST   23 km (14 miles); 13 km walks
AREA 19   Merioneth ME
                             Map 124; 1″ 116; 2½″ SH *52, 62*

The western side of the Rhinog mountain block shows the characteristic of cultural unity with Snowdonia already noted in Area 18. It is only lightly dissected by its pattern of direct drainage to the coast, which allows easy passage on foot from N. to S., though access by road to the upland terrain is limited. Barmouth and the coastal strip through Dyffryn and Llanbedr to Harlech have become a place of holiday pilgrimage, and thus abound in instant accommodation.

Behind Egryn Abbey, 5 km N. of Barmouth, is a group of sites which can be included in a walk of 5 km from the coast road. First, at *600 201*, in an area of good cultivation terraces, but itself poorly preserved, is a *round hut* with a yard and outer enclosure, all concentrically arranged on a level shelf. At *616 203* is a *cairn-circle* 7.8 m in diameter, excavated in 1919 by O. G. S. Crawford, a pioneer in field archaeology who at that time was already recording metric measurements. Finding no trace of burial within the ring of outward-leaning stones he concluded that all original internal features had been destroyed when the cairn material was robbed. Many of the large stones have now gone.

Carneddau Hengwm
HM pp. 9–15   *613 205* ME
The two long cairns lying side by side on open moorland differ in size and in such detail as can still be made out after considerable robbing for the building of field walls, of which one crosses the south cairn. The south cairn is 46 m long and contains a ruined chamber of portal dolmen type at the E. end, which still stood in the late XVIII century. There is a lateral chamber on the N. and some upright stones at the W. suggest a squared end, which could belong to an enlargment with stylistic features of the Severn-Cotswold tradition. The smaller, north cairn repeats this possibility, having at its E. end the upright stones of what may have been two lateral chambers back to back, while some dry walling on the N. seems to be a remnant of a defining revetment. The capstone at the W. end rests on cairn material, and is clearly displaced.

Pen y Dinas
HM p. 150   *606 209* ME
A small, rounded spur overlooking the Afon Egryn from the N. is encircled by a ditch and stone-faced rampart 4.5 m wide at the base, as shown by Crawford's excavation in 1919. It is particularly massive at the sunken entrance, where a timber bridge can be assumed. The approach road from the N. is clear, and flanked on the W. by an outwork forming a second rampart. Two rectangular huts by the road are presumably medieval, and though the original fort can be seen as a small Iron Age refuge, it might well have been used also in early medieval times. Below the fort, on a shelf above a steep drop to the stream, is a strongly **enclosed hut** with a terraced approach path.

Corsygedol Hut-Group
HM p. 202   *604 230* ME
Not in good condition, but informative when excavated in 1956. In the N.W. corner of a system of terraced fields, it consists of two huts 8 m in diameter and a rectangular room (possibly the 'dairy' as at Braich y Gornel in Area 4), with orthostatic facing to the walls. An oak bowl was

found, indicating what was evidently the native alternative to earthen-ware; a few sherds of pottery indicate a date in the II century A.D.

Corsygedol Cromlech
HM p. 19   *602 228* ME

The long cairn here is of irregular shape owing to robbing, but can be traced to a length of 26 m, with a ruined chamber in the N.E. end. The capstone rests on one of two remaining uprights, probably part of a portal entrance. The local name Coetan Arthur is a common one, which ascribes to a legendary hero the great strength needed for such a mighty work.

This is the starting point for a walk of some 8 km on the flanks of the Afon Ysgethin.

Craig y Dinas
HM p. 158   *624 230* ME

A rocky spur standing out from Moelfre in a bend of the river has been fortified at its tip by a carefully built stone wall over 2 m thick, now somewhat obscured by a modern wall, but still visible to more than 1 m in height at its outer face above the steep drop to the S.E. Some double facing in places is for strength, and is not an indication of two periods of construction. This is a small, family-size fort, but the only visible huts are four outside on the S.E. There is an oblique entrance way past an out-turned rampart end, flanked by two extra walls.

On a saddle to the N.N.E. at *625 229* are four low **cairns** about 6 m in diameter, one topped by a standing stone, another having a retaining circle of stones.

Hengwm Circles
HM p. 35   *616 213* ME

There are two circles close to the track here in a small enclosure, 37 m and 33 m in diameter and 30 m apart. They have lost many stones to the field walls and are now hard to make out, but sockets were found by Crawford in 1919 in the larger. The embankment of the smaller, northern circle had stones 5 yards apart, according to Pennant in the XVIII century; a grave-like pit lay within, and a fire-pit contained a necked beaker. The larger circle also had a beaker, in one of the stone sockets.

Dyffryn Long Cairn
HM p. 17   *588 228* ME

An important excavation and restoration here in 1961–2 revealed a two-stage structural sequence. A completely closed portal dolmen in its own round cairn was included after only a short interval in a wedge-shaped long cairn, which had a second chamber near the E. end. Pottery from a pit in the V-shaped forecourt of the first chamber dates the whole sequence probably as early as 3000 B.C. In State care, open always without charge; easily accessible behind Dyffryn school. The cairn lies in an area of some of the finest Iron Age cultivation terraces in the county, visible on the hillsides above.

Further megalithic sites in the district include **Bron-y-foel Isaf Cairn** (*608 246*), displaying a portal with blocking stone in position. The capstone leans on one side stone, and the cairn has been reduced to 18 m by 9 m by robbing. In **Llanbedr Church** (*585 269*) is a natural stone slab bearing seven turns of a spiral groove 0.3 m across altogether, a sample of megalithic art from an unidentified site, but clearly akin to the decoration of Barclodiad y Gawres (Area 1).

Gwern Einion Burial Chamber

HM p. 15   *587 286* ME

A good example of a portal dolmen which has survived through its incorporation in a field wall, though its cairn has practically vanished. The capstone typically slopes sharply back from the portal, which retains its blocking stone.

THE MAWDDACH   45 km (28 miles)
AREA 20   Merioneth ME
                 Map 124; 1″ 116; 2½″ SH *61, 71, 72*

The cold north face of the second great mountain of Wales dominates the estuary of the Mawddach, which is fed by two short valleys from the rocky enclave behind the Rhinogs. Prehistoric habitation was sparse in those inner regions, where today forestry has been added to the only other viable farming activity, the rearing of sheep. The broad shelf at about 200 m below Cader Idris itself carries the greatest variety of archaeological sites in the area; the rest are dispersed along the valleys, where the scenery is a bonus to anyone using the market town of Dolgellau as a touring base.

Moel Offrwm Hillfort
HM p. 141   *749 210* ME

Sited neatly on its own self-contained summit, the main fortification is polygonal, about 100 m across, and contains several levelled hut platforms, suggesting use as a permanent settlement rather than as a place of refuge. Round the northern half of its circuit the single stone rampart lies scattered down the slope, perhaps deliberately. In the S.W. quarter it is better preserved, while across the neck of a small spur to the S.E., flanking the entrance which has been somewhat adapted in modern times, a double rampart can be made out. The spur was also lightly fortified as an outwork.

On a rocky knoll to the S. overlooking **Nannau** at *748 206*, is a small fort containing a single hut site. The double facing of the dry-built rampart can be clearly seen in places, between outcrops which were cleverly incorporated in its line on the south side. The entrance was probably more oblique than the present passage suggests.

The fortified enclosure on **Foel Faner** (*733 204*), the southern summit of the ridge of Foel Cynwch, is a simple, irregular oval with an overlapping entrance at the N.E. corner, to the W. of which the stone wall faces are well preserved. Though it commands an impressive view, the position is naturally weak by comparison with its neighbour to the E.

Brithdir Roman Fortlet
RFW p. 130   *772 189* ME

A comparatively recent discovery, this is a small but strategically placed post in the Roman road network (Fig. 12). A level platform on a slight summit can be seen from the modern lane, which approximates to the original Roman road striking N.E. towards Caer Gai (Area 14). It was probably just over 50 m square, but has suffered greatly from the plough.

Craig y Castell
HM p. 160   *694 158* ME

The steep crags on the N. of this small eminence needed no further defence, but a dry-stone rampart, showing multiple construction for stability, was added on the other sides. At the S.E. it swung round a prominent boss to form a bastion flanking the entrance passage through a natural gully. It remains an open question whether such small forts were created solely for refuge, or contained timber dwellings that have left no trace above ground.

The grassy moorland through which the open road approached *Llyn Cregennen* from the S.E. contains several cairns which may be hard to locate (*65 13, 66 13*) but the stone called **Carreg y Big** standing at *662 138* is a more prominent indicator of Bronze Age activity on the mountainside. The cairn circle near the medieval **Llys Bradwen** (*652 139*) has been badly disturbed; 10 stones survive, but only three lie on the probable rim of the cairn.

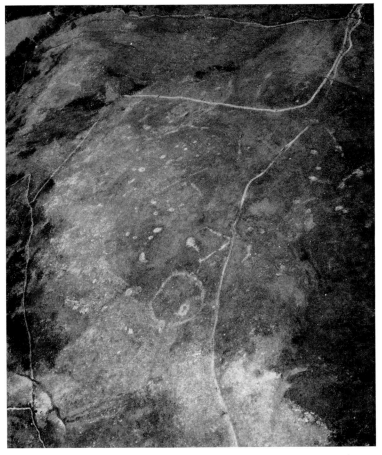

Plate 14. Bryn Seward (Area 20): scattered settlement remains of the Iron Age. *Photo: J. K. S. St. Joseph.*

As in Area 18 a succession of **standing stones** by the trackway which traverses the mountainside from Llwyngwril has been claimed as of Bronze Age origin. There is ample reason to accept their early date, but one may perhaps see them not so much as deliberate markers of the route, but as having been so placed in a prominent wayside position for less practical, perhaps spiritual reasons. There are nine stones from *601 103* to *626 117*, ranging from 1 m to 2.4 m high, with another at *651 133* and Carreg y Big (above) completing the sequence. Near **Cyfanned** too, at *634 122*, there is a good cairn with an elaborate kerb 9 m in diameter, while two simpler ones are near the track at *624 117*, and one at *622 116*.

Iron Age settlement along the same track has left several enclosures in a ruinous state, such as the one at *634 122* measuring 34 m by 41 m, with traces of a hut within, and another round hut in a circular paddock at *Bryn Seward* (*623 117*), with many scattered huts and field walls nearby (Plate 14).

THE DYFI   110 km (68 miles)
AREA 21   Merioneth ME, Montgomeryshire MY
    Map 124, 135, 136; 1″ 127, 128; 2½″ SH 50, 60, 70, 80, 90, SN 69, 79, 89

In summer the Mawddach and Dyfi valleys bring the English Midlanders in force to the Cambrian Coast in parallel streams. The narrow mountain block between their estuaries is more finely dissected in the same W.S.W. direction, but their inland tributaries spring from wider sectors of the backbone of Wales. The variety of archaeological sites is limited by the topography to Bronze Age burial and ritual monuments on the remote moorland, Iron Age defensive works on small summits near the more fertile valleys, and vestiges of the transient Roman attempt to control the subjugated natives with their network of roads and military outposts. For convenience one may choose Machynlleth as a base, and enjoy its austere charm and its deep-seated faith in its right to become the parliamentary capital of Wales; Aberdovey and Towyn have their own seaside attraction as alternatives.

In Machynlleth itself a stone pillar known as **Maen Llwyd** (*752 008*), in an open space near the main street, is 1.7 m high, and probably of Bronze Age date. The road westward along the N. side of the Dyfi

estuary leads past **Pennal Roman Fort** (*705 001*), in a position typically on a low spur above the flood plain, near the lowest reasonable
crossing point of the river (Fig. 12). It has been very much damaged by
ploughing, and finds have been only casual and not very informative.
There is a suggestion of stone construction, and of a bath house on the
S. side.

In **Towyn Church** (*588 009*) is an VIII century memorial, notable
for the earliest use of Welsh on stone. Two successive inscriptions, as
reinterpreted by the late Sir Ifor Williams, commemorate 'Ceinrwy,
wife of Addian, close to Bud and Meirchiaw'; and 'Cun, wife of Celyn:
grief and loss remain'.

Talygarreg Fort
HM p. 167   *574 036* ME
On a prominent hilltop looking down on the coastal plain, this is a

Plate 15. Craig yr Aderyn (Area 21): a small Iron Age stronghold perched
above the valley. *Photo: J. K. S. St. Joseph.*

very small fortification consisting of a double line of stony banks abutting on a steep cliff at the N.E. At the S. end a strong bank with a rock-cut ditch has been added to a small, semicircular internal structure in an unusual way.

Craig yr Aderyn
Pl. 15; *HM* p. 142   *644 069* ME
A striking natural feature which almost defied fortification to any effective purpose. An L-shaped bank ends on the S. and E. where the slopes become precipitous. The same idea was repeated for added strength in a second stage on the E. as a massive stone wall with an inturned entrance fairly clearly preserved.

East of Machynlleth is another **Maen Llwyd** at *828 005*, standing 1.8 m high, at a low altitude by comparison with most of the Bronze Age sites here. Near the road to Dylife, after the long climb to the edge of the plateau, are two good barrows on *Brynyfedwen* at *841 953* and *843 954*, one of which yielded a good specimen of a barbed-and-tanged arrowhead. Many more of these flint weapon tips have been found in the peat around Llyn Bugeilyn and Glaslyn, lost there at a time when drier conditions encouraged good hunting for the Bronze Age shepherds.

Pen y Crogbren
RFW p. 143   *855 934* MY
The name ('Gallows-top') refers to the execution here of an XVIII century murderer from the then thriving lead-mining village of Dylife. Though there is no direct evidence on the point, the construction of this small, rectangular earthwork by the Romans in the early II century could have been occasioned by the need to protect their own exploitation of lead.

Cerrig Caerau and **Lled Croen-yr-ych** (*903 005*) are two stone circles which occupy a broad saddle at a natural meeting place of upland routes. The eight stones remaining of the fourteen or so that originally made up the first circle, 19 m in diameter, all lie prostrate. The second site, 130 m to the N., is also disturbed; five boulders remain, but hollows marking the positions of ten others make up a circle of 25 m diameter, irregularly spaced. Some ceremonial purpose can be assumed for both circles.

PLYNLIMON WEST   58 km (36 miles)
AREA 22   Cardiganshire CD, Montgomeryshire MY
                      Map 135; 1″ 127; 2½″ SN *58, 67–69, 77, 78*

Rising near each other in the same mountain core as the Severn and
Wye, the Ystwyth and Rheidol reach the sea together at Aberystwyth,
a focal point of the Cardigan Bay coast, where leisure and learning have
flourished side by side for over a century. The structure of the land
runs east and west, making movement difficult between north and south
from Roman to modern times. The coastline, exposed to severe weather
and away from the western sea route, was not a great attraction to
early settlers, but the fort of Pen Dinas stands out as the beachhead of
Iron Age immigrants. The Ceredigion Museum recently established
has few early relics, but there are two excellent examples of decorated
Celtic memorial stones in **Llanbadarn Church** (*599 810*).

Pen Dinas
Fig. 18; *PEW* p. 144   *584 805* CD
The twin summits and the Wellington Monument make a familiar
landmark today for seafarers, and it was no surprise that the excavations
of 1933–7 revealed an origin in south-west Britain for the hill's first
inhabitants. Both summits were separately fortified, the north first, then
the south in two phases, with two main gateways. The whole was then
enclosed in a single circuit, with three reconstructions of the new main
entrance on the saddle between. The whole history of the site is probably to be fitted into the last three centuries B.C.

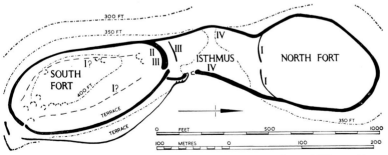

Figure 18. Pen Dinas (Area 22): the development of the hillfort. *After
R.C.A.M., Crown Copyright.*

H

Hen Gaer   *633 844* CD
A good example of a family-size fortification, as distinct from the tribal refuge; to be compared with Henllan (Area 39). It is strongly defended by a bank and rock-cut ditch; the flattened mound opposite the entrance is part of the defensive scheme, not an earlier barrow. **Caer Llettyllwyd** (*651 882*) is about the same size as Hen Gaer and presumably similar in purpose, though there are suggestions of two constructional periods.

The crossing of the Dyfi chosen by the Romans for their road south from Pennal (Area 21) is lost, though the early medieval castle mound at *687 969* is a likely indicator of former control at this point. From Furnace a lane ascends steeply to the mountainside using what must have been the *Roman route* for most of the distance to Talybont (Fig. 12). An abandoned section at *683 947* shows a Roman directness on a gradient too severe for modern traffic. On the way *Bedd Taliesin* (*671 912*) is not far above the road, but in poor condition now, with its central cist robbed; the name fancifully puts into a Bronze Age grave the early medieval bard whose home was at the foot of the mountain.

From Talybont a small road leads over the first mountain barrier to the Nant-y-moch hydro-electric reservoir. Before the water level rose in 1962 a ring cairn at *Abercamddwr* (*754 866*) yielded an urn from a

Plate 16. Penllwyn (Area 22): a Bronze Age encrusted urn of Irish type. *Photo: National Museum of Wales.*

central pit, and the headless, dismembered remains of a child burnt in a small hollow. Good mountain cairns within reach include two at *776 898* on *Banc Llechwedd-mawr*, and two on *Carn Gwilym* (*792 908*). More accessible cairns lie close to the road at **Lle'rneuaddau** (*759 853* and *755 847*), while the group of three at **Hirnant** (*753 839*) includes one with a prominent retaining circle. Note also **Garn Lwyd** by the road at *752 833*. West of the Rheidol the summit cairn of *Disgwylfa Fawr* (*737 847*) was sadly wrecked as recently as 1937 in the name of archaeology. At the centre of the stone heap were two hollowed tree trunks, 2.5 m and 1.1 m long, both waterlogged and so well preserved. The smaller one contained cremated bones, a flint blade and a food vessel of Irish type. A remarkable encrusted urn from *Penllwyn* (*653 803*, Plate 16) confirms the Irish influence later in the Bronze Age.

Ysbyty Cynfyn Circle
SCW p. 127   *752 791* CD
In an interesting association of pagan and Christian structures, an embanked circle has been adapted to form the churchyard enclosure by the addition of a wall on the outer slope. Two stones under 2 m high have probably been moved for use as gateposts; another pair in the wall may still be in place, but a fifth on the N. is clearly so, standing 3.4 m high. No ditch is in evidence, and none may ever have existed, if this circle followed the type of Meini Gywr (Area 40).

Where the River Ystwyth levels out near **Trawscoed** (*670 727*) a Roman fort was discovered in 1959, evidently sited to control the river crossing at a point roughly half way between Pennal and Llanio (Fig. 12). The modern B4575 road passes diagonally through the site, of which the 2 ha rectangle is now only recognisable from the slight swelling of the turf and timber rampart. Excavation showed this to have been increased in width at some time, though the whole history of the site probably did not extend beyond the I century A.D. The *road* southwards is traceable as it crosses forest and farmland for 8 km, and can be easily seen where it joins the A485 (see Area 38). Northwards the line is mainly followed by modern lanes, with typical Roman engineering to be seen in zigzags at *669 748* and *646 827*.

Gaer Fawr   *649 719* CD
The fort occupies the whole of an oval summit, with two banks widely spaced for some of the circuit; the outer, perhaps unfinished, takes the form of a massive terrace on the N. side, reminiscent of Pen Dinas. A

different approach to defence is seen at **Penffrwdllwyd** (*709 688*), where a cliff on the W. provided a strong natural defence. The circuit was completed by a semicircular pair of banks, the outer having a ditch, and a further bank on the N., facing the more level ground there. At least one hut platform can be seen inside.

5 SOUTH CENTRAL RIVERS
The Wye and Usk

Figure 19. Llanwrthwl (Breck.): a twisted bar of solid gold wound into an armlet, but probably originally a neck ornament. Brecknock Museum (Area 27). Scale 1:2. *After photo: National Museum of Wales.*

THE UPPER WYE
72 km (45 miles)

AREA 23   Cardiganshire CD, Montgomeryshire MY, Radnorshire RA

Map 135, 136; 1″ 127, 128; 2½″ SN *78, 88, 96, 97,* SO *07*

The best main road to Cardigan Bay from the S.E. runs up the Wye for 50 km, leaving it at last only just S. of its source in Plynlimon. The river and its tributaries have cut deeply, with the help of ice, leaving a rocky landscape of great scenic beauty between smooth stretches of mountain. The conflict of forest versus sheep occupies the human arena today, with the further question of who really owns the water that the English take for their cities. Rhayader, while retaining its original market town status, has survived and has thrived on such economic and political issues, to become a useful summer tourist centre.

Archaeological sites are widely scattered and not numerous, but full advantage can be taken of the scenery by starting with a circuit of the Elan Valley lakes. On a minor diversion towards the Claerwen Dam, a stiff climb of the hillside leads to an alignment of five stones on **Rhos y Gelynen** (*902 629*), three of them small at 0.7 m high, but one is a slab 1.5 m high, and one a pillar measuring 2.3 m. These are presumed to be connected in some way with Bronze Age ritual practices, including burial. There are several cairns on the mountain tops, mostly far from the road, to which visits are a matter of personal enterprise.

Clap-yr-arian
Pl. 17; *INV* No. 398–9   *936 699* RA

On the mountain edge, and reasonably accessible from the old coach

Plate 17. Clap-yr-arian (Area 23): a battle-axe of Preseli 'bluestone' from a Bronze Age cairn. Scale 2:3. *Photo: National Museum of Wales.*

route to Aberystwyth, one stone cairn remains out of a prominent pair. From it came a perfect specimen of a battle-axe made of the well-known spotted blue dolerite of Preseli (Area 41). The occupant of this grave might well have belonged to one of the groups of beaker-using people who transported the 'bluestones' to Stonehenge.

Y Maen Serth (*944 698*) above a cliff not far to the E. is a stone slab over 2 m high which may well have a Bronze Age origin, though the cross on one side of it may be thought to support the tradition that this was the site of the murder of one Einion Clud in the XII century A.D.

Esgairperfedd Marching Camp
RFW p. 126   *927 699* RA
South of the coach road, near the head of its steepest climb, is the site chosen by a Roman military unit for a temporary camp while on the move. There is an entrance 7.6 m wide in each of its four straight sides, which enclose some 6 ha. This would have been a possible route between Castell Collen (Area 24) and the Trawscoed fort (Area 22), perhaps joining another road from Cae Gaer (below) further W.

Plynlimon Cairns   *789 869* etc. CD, MY
From Eisteddfa Gurig the ascent of Pumlumon (its correct name) is

not severe. Two stone cairns at the summit are only the first of a series of seven which can be reached in a 5 km walk to the N.E., for which the 1-inch map is an adequate guide. All have been pulled about in ancient treasure-seeking greed or modern ignorance, and may not be thought worthy of the exercise. A number of barbed-and-tanged arrowheads have been found on these ridges, testimony to Bronze Age hunting as in Area 21.

Cae Gaer

RFW p. 132   *824 819* MY

In an area left unplanted by the Forestry Commission, best approached on foot from the main road, this fortlet is a parallelogram, perhaps through a Roman surveyor's miscalculation, but possibly to suit the awkward little plateau on which it is sited. Of its two gateways, that on the S. has been eroded away. Excavation in 1913 revealed a turf rampart 5 m wide containing posts 10 cm thick at intervals of 0.6 m, and a shallow ditch 2 m wide. There were no datable finds to confirm the presumed Roman origin.

Contrasting with the summit cairns of Plynlimon and the ridges flanking the Wye valley, there are several in secluded valley situations in the Rhayader area, none of them outstanding, but reasonably accessible: *012 755*, known as *The Mount*, or Bedd Garmon, in a river bend. *990 740*, two near the *Afon Marteg* in a small plantation; one was excavated in 1961, revealing carbonised planks and cremated bones. *983 724*, known as *Crugyn*, dominating a bend in the river. *985 684* and *991 686* near *Downfield*; two undisturbed mounds at either end of a low spur between streams.

THE IRFON AND IEITHON   58 km (36 miles)
AREA 24   Brecknock BR, Radnorshire RA
            Map 147, 148; 1″ 128, 141; 2½″ SN *94–96*, SO *05, 06, 16*

Two major tributaries join the Wye near Builth Wells, a natural market town at the meeting of half a dozen valley and mountain routes. One of the two surviving railways of mid-Wales follows the Irfon and Ieithon in turn from the head of the Tywi Vale, and it is no surprise to find that the Romans too focused their road system on a major fort in the same area. Llandrindod Wells, a former spa town and now the administrative centre of Radnorshire, is the best choice as an archaeological base, but the whole region is becoming very conscious of its potential for the mobile holiday-maker.

Llandrindod Wells Museum
Temple St.   *060 611* RA
Under the joint auspices of the town and the Radnorshire Society, the museum is affiliated to the National Museum of Wales, and serves basically as a repository for the Roman material from Castell Collen, but there is a small number of prehistoric finds from the region as well. Particularly noteworthy is a primitive dug-out canoe found in the River Ieithon in 1929, where it had been moored at a landing-stage behind a breakwater. These is no reason to give it a date earlier than medieval.

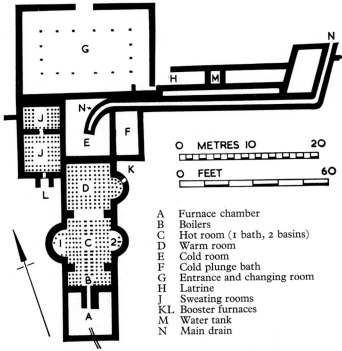

A   Furnace chamber
B   Boilers
C   Hot room (1 bath, 2 basins)
D   Warm room
E   Cold room
F   Cold plunge bath
G   Entrance and changing room
H   Latrine
J   Sweating rooms
KL Booster furnaces
M   Water tank
N   Main drain

Figure 20. Castell Collen (Area 24): the garrison bath-house attached to the Roman fort. *After L. Alcock.*

Castell Collen

Fig. 20; *RFW* p. 74   *055 628* RA

Securely sited by the River Ieithon, on rising ground between streams, this Roman fort has been shown in excavations of 1911–13 and 1954–7 to have been developed through four phases, with periods of abandonment. For the first two phases (late I and mid II centuries) an apparently detached ditch is all that remains of the W. end of the fort, which was reduced for the last two phases (early III and early IV centuries) from about 2 ha to the 1.44 ha seen today, thus halving the troop accommodation to 500 infantry. The originally central headquarters buildings occupied the same position throughout, though timber was replaced by stone, as in the defences. The bath house to the S. is a good example of what was always an important adjunct of a permanent military station.

The *Roman route* to the S.W. (Fig. 12) can be picked up at *046 625*, where it joins the present line of the A4081, and leads eventually to Beulah. The recently discovered fort at **Caerau** (*923 502*) was a staging post on the way to Llandovery (Area 36). Its 1.7 ha were reduced to 1.2 ha by the time of its abandonment in the mid II century. Its turf-and-timber construction seems never to have been replaced with stonework; the S.W. end is obscured by a medieval motte and modern buildings.

Another stretch of road heading in the same general direction, but on the E. of the Ieithon across Llandrindod Common, can be seen as a faint ridge, passing W. of an important group of *practice camps*. These were simply exercises in defensive construction for the troops, of no strategic significance. Of the 18 known in 1811, 14 survive (some only as cropmarks). All except one have four entrances with covering banks (*tutuli*) and vary in size from 14 m to over 30 m square. The best four can be seen at *054 602*, where two lie on each side of a lane leading W. from the main road.

South-east of Llandrindod the hills present an intricate relief of ridges and spurs, with many ideal situations for fortification, of which the Iron Age population took full advantage. **Careg Wiber Bank** (*084 595*) is a promontory fort with a single rampart and a sharply inturned entrance at one end. The site overlooks the head of a short tributary of the Ieithon on the W. On an isolated hill which is part of the same terrain, but cut off in a bend of the river, is **Cefnllys Castle** (*089 615*), best approached from the N. The prehistoric enclosure here seems to have been used as the bailey of a medieval castle, which crowns its S.W. end.

Castle Bank   *087 561* RA

There are two separate forts here, both of contour type. The first lay on the southward extension of the ridge, and had only one defensive bank. The second occupied the N. end of the ridge, so that the first was eventually used as its outer enclosure. This was also univallate, with a counterscarp bank at the steep N. end and an entrance with thickened ends to its bank terminals at the S. end.

A walk of 5 km along the Carneddau ridge will take in three good hillforts, and will pass *cairns* at *066 541* and elsewhere on the top. **Cwmberwyn Camp** (*073 548*), on a spur pointing S.E., small in area, is defended only by a single rampart, which becomes double on the level ground facing N.W., with a formidable ditch between. **Caer Einion** (*063 531*) is sited on a spur similar to the last, but with more cliffs and crags to form the basis of the defensive scheme, which relies on the isolation afforded by a saddle on the N.W. The inner stone rampart has a slightly inturned entrance. **Gaer Fawr** (*058 531*) is a more formidable fort than the last two, in a superior position on the S. spur of the main ridge. It has multiple defences, with an entrance of oblique barbican type, enclosing more than 1 ha.

The descent to the Royal Welsh Show ground at *Llanelwedd* leads along the top of rapidly expanding quarries, which have already eaten into an area containing several interesting long mounds (*051 523*). When one of these was excavated recently in the belief that it was a medieval rabbit warren, it yielded neolithic pottery from beneath one end; but it would be rash to claim it as a neolithic long barrow on these grounds alone.

Cwm Cefn-y-gaer   *114 698* and *121 699* RA

Before returning to Llandrindod a sortie to the N. affords a chance to examine a contrasting pair of hillforts on adjacent summits. The west fort is multivallate and small, with widely spaced banks following the contours. The entrance has been largely obliterated. The east fort is univallate, twice as big at 4 ha, built of stone and has a sharply inturned entrance.

RADNOR FOREST   40 km (25 miles)
AREA 25   Radnorshire RA
                      Map 148; 1″ 128, 129; 2½″ SO *15, 16, 25–27*

The heights of Radnor Forest are wild now, and must have had little to
offer to prehistoric man but game and grazing in the Bronze Age.
Certainly there are few traces of early agricultural penetration W. of
Offa's Dyke, which was well sited to establish the best land as Mercian
territory in a later age. All the archaeology of this region is easily
reached from Knighton, one of the natural 'gateway' towns of Wales. A
visit to *Hereford* and its **Museum** would be appropriate while exploring
this part of the borderland.

Offa's Dyke

Figs. 12, 21; *OD* pp. 139–48   *283 720* etc. RA
About 20 km of the dyke now lie in Shropshire, between Area 16 and
the River Teme at Knighton. The dyke crosses the Teme and Lugg
valleys within the present Area, passing into Herefordshire near
Kington. The whole of this southern-central section was probably the
first to be completed, once its line had been established by treaty, and it
exhibits great skill on the part of its engineers, who maintained a
constant western outlook in spite of the complications of the topography.
The efforts of enthusiasts in the Border Country have now secured
footpath rights over virtually the whole length of the dyke, but for those
who prefer an intermittent inspection it can be seen at *283 720* as it
climbs over the golf course, continuing over Hawthorn Hill from the
B4355 at *282 688*. Its zigzag course S. of the Lugg crosses lanes at *272
651, 269 639*, and E. of Evenjobb, with a final climb across the W. end of
Burfa Hill. It is worth remarking here that along the whole course of the
Mercian frontier through Herefordshire, and as far as the last ten miles
of the Wye, Offa's Dyke was actually constructed only in short stretches
where Saxon settlements had penetrated the natural forest of the region.

    In crossing the Lugg valley, the dyke passes the site of a small Roman
fort at *Discoed (268 653)*, spotted from the air in 1967. Its character is
still not fully understood, but it probably served as a control point on a
route leading W. towards Castell Collen (Area 24). On the hill further
S. is a small Iron Age fort, **Castle Ring** (*266 636*), distinguished by the
strength of its single rampart with counterscarp bank, as the plateau
siting demanded. It has two simple, opposed entrances.

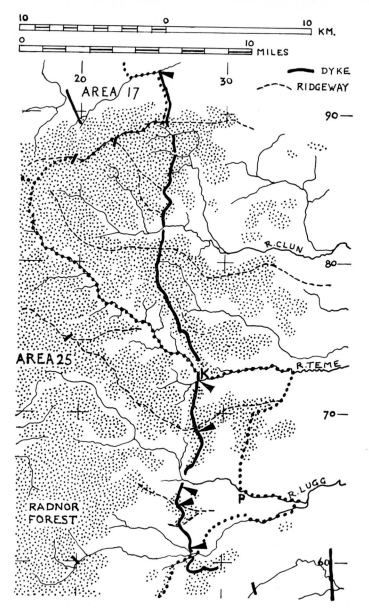

Figure 21. Offa's Dyke (Area 25): its course across the valleys of the southern Marches. Arrows indicate convenient viewing points. *After Sir Cyril Fox.*

Burfa Camp
INV No. 163   *284 610* RA

The whole of Burfa Bank has been too thickly forested. Though some trees have been removed from the complicated barbican entrance on the S., it is still difficult to follow the defences, which are multiple all round, doubtless covering a complicated history of adaptation through several periods. The slanting approach from the N.W. is particularly well defended.

The Four Stones
INV No. 615b   *245 608* RA

These are clearly glacial erratic boulders, but they have been selected and placed with flat faces towards the centre of the space between them. They are hardly typical of a megalithic tomb, but must rank as a prehistoric setting, even though their purpose remains enigmatic.

The broad valley between Walton and Old Radnor contains many cropmarks of circles and Roman sites not yet explored. There are also several Bronze Age barrows in the cultivated fields, which have produced their share of surface finds; two N.E. of *Harpton Court* (*244 600*) are close to the road. The dyke called **Ditch Bank** at *197 600* W. of New Radnor occupies only the bottom of the valley, but is probably part of the Mercian system, intended as an outlying protection for a deeper penetration of Welsh territory.

THE MIDDLE WYE   42 km (26 miles)
AREA 26   Brecknock BR, Radnorshire RA
                   Map 161; 1″ 141; 2½″ SO *12, 13, 23, 24*

The Wye bends N.E. to leave the mountain zone and Wales at Hay; its tributaries in this middle section are short, owing to the closeness of the hills on either side, but there is an important area of comparatively low hills between the Wye and the Usk which appealed to colonising farmers of two prehistoric phases. Neolithic chambered long cairns here, and in Area 28, represent the furthest spread into Wales of the Severn-Cotswold culture, while hilltop fortifications testify to the defensive needs of the Iron Age population. There are several pleasantly located hotels, both in villages and countryside; and a thriving holiday centre at Llangorse, catering primarily for yachtsmen, pony-trekkers and walkers.

At *Llangorse Lake* (*129 269*) in 1925 was found the dug-out canoe to be seen in the Brecknock Museum (Area 27). Though of primitive type it may be only medieval in date, used for access to the island near the N. shore for fishing and similar purposes. There is, however, some reason to suspect an Iron Age 'crannog' here, artificially improved with stakes as a lake-dwelling like those at Glastonbury and Meare in Somerset.

Hillis Fort   *114 327* BR

The oval hilltop was enclosed by two sizable ramparts, best seen on the W. side. The layout of a deeply inturned entrance at the S. end is clearly preserved, while another gateway at the N.E. made intelligent use of rock outcrops as bastions. The N. end is inexplicably weakly defended on the ridge, but the absence of clear defences on half of the E. side is due to destruction by agriculture. The ridge across the middle seems never to have been used as a rampart line, though it looks like one.

Fortification for military rather than domestic defence takes the familiar Roman form at *Clyro* (*227 435*), though little can be seen in ground-level inspection. A broad hillock overlooking the Wye was incorporated in the rectangular layout, unusually large at 10.4 ha and almost certainly belonging only to the early campaigns of *c.* A.D. 60, when either half a legion or several auxiliary units might have been stationed here.

Penywyrlod Long Cairn
PCT p. 213   *225 398* BR
A comparatively small cairn at 18.3 m long, with a rectangular chamber in its N.E. end, consisting of four uprights, but no extant capstone; another chamber lies to one side at the S.W. end. Partial excavation in 1920 did little to add any constructional detail, but this tomb is clearly somewhere near the end of a natural devolution from the classic Severn-Cotswold type found nearer to the Bristol Channel.

Ffostill Long Cairns
PCT p. 213   *179 349* BR
An interesting pair of chambered tombs which have points of difference as well as resemblance. The better-preserved south one has a single chamber in the form of a gallery just over 3 m long in its N.E. end, lined

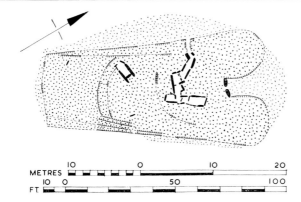

Figure 22. Pipton Long Cairn (Area 26): an elaborate constructional history revealed by excavation. *After H. N. Savory.*

by ten uprights which supported the two displaced capstones. The slightly larger north cairn lies more directly east–west. Its main chamber at the E. end is wrecked, but it had another small one in the centre of the N. side, and possibly a third at the S.W. corner. Both cairns were inadequately excavated in 1921–3.

More recently a properly conducted excavation in farmland above *Pipton (160 373)* revealed a wealth of detail about the construction of another of these Brecknockshire tombs (Fig. 22). It was typically wedge-shaped, squared at the narrow end and divided at the broad end by a forecourt between rounded 'horns'. Indications of lateness in the series are the pretence of the dummy portal, the hiding of the true entrance of the complicated gallery at the side, and the change from the regularity of the transepted plan of Parc Cwm (Area 35). A second chamber without an entrance passage contained seven piles of disarticulated bones, evidently collected from an interim resting place. The dry-stone revetments were finely built, and were carefully covered soon afterwards with a deliberate mask of clay and stones. The whole tomb has many points of resemblance to the Tŷ-isaf cairn of Area 28.

THE UPPER USK   79 km (49 miles)
AREA 27   Brecknock BR
        Map 160; 1″ 140, 141; 2½″ SN *82, 83, 92, 93*, SO *02, 03, 11, 12*

Water engineers have their eye firmly fixed on the Usk basin as a new
source of supply for the south coast towns, for a great quantity of rainfall is collected by the tributaries which draw together here from
Fforest Fawr on the S. and Mynydd Eppynt on the N. The threat to
good valley farmland is shared by the important centre of Roman
activity at Brecon Gaer, where several mountain and valley routes meet,
in a different pattern from today's communications. There are some
good hilltop refuges of the pre-Roman agricultural population on the
intervening ridges, while the higher mountain areas had their own
limited use, for pasturage in the drier Bronze Age and for campaign and
movement by the Roman army.

   With historical repetition some of the more interesting archaeology
N.W. of Brecon is inaccessible because of the more dangerous military
activities of the present day, but there is still plenty of room on the
Beacons for the pony-trekker and the determined walker. Brecon itself
is a historic town deserving consideration as a base for touring, if one
of the more isolated hotels of country and riverside is not preferred.

The Brecknock Museum, Brecon   *045 285* BR

Founded in 1928 by the Brecknock Society, the museum is now affiliated to the National Museum of Wales, and is administered by the
County Council. With a dug-out canoe from Llangorse (Area 26) as the
centre-piece, the general collection from the region represents all
periods with casual finds, including copies of the Late Bronze Age
bracelets from Llanwrthwl (Fig. 19). More important, perhaps, are
exhibits of excavation material from sites such as the chambered tombs
of the area, and Brecon Gaer. There are several casts or originals of
inscribed stones ranging from the V century Latin and ogam memorial
to Maccutrenus Salicidunus found at Trecastle (*880 290*), and a VI
century one in Latin only to Nennius, son of Victorinus, brought from
the roadside at Scethrog (*110 248*), to a X century pillar cross from
Maesmynis (*012 476*).

Plate 18. Brecon Gaer (Area 27): the south gate of the II century fort, as exposed in excavations. *Photo: National Museum of Wales.*

Brecon Gaer

Pl. 18; *RFW* p. 48   *002 297* BR

On a low spur overlooking the confluence of the Usk and the Yscir, the Romans established a key fort after the completion of their conquest in about A.D. 80, to house a garrison of 500 cavalry. Excavations in 1924–5 showed that the original earth and timber defences with two ditches were replaced by stonework *c.* 140. The headquarters buildings were also elaborated at this time, and a bath house was added in the barrack area, instead of in the usual external position. Purposeful military occupation may not have lasted beyond 200, but the fort seems to have been used again towards 300. There was also an extensive civil settlement outside the N. gate. The S. and W. gates are preserved as they were found, and there are good stretches of wall visible, topped in places by medieval work. In State care, open always without charge; a pamphlet is available.

Of the Roman roads radiating from the Gaer (Fig. 12), that towards

l

Coelbren (Area 34) is the most accessible, and can be seen as a slightly raised *agger* across **Mynydd Illtud** at *968 265*. **Bedd Illtud** at *974 264* is a fair example of a simple Bronze Age ring cairn.

Twyn-y-gaer   *990 280* BR

A small hillfort in a commanding position, but never elaborated from its original single-ramparted form with inturned entrance. Outside on the E. are some large specimens of pillow mounds, probably rabbit warrens of post-medieval date, not to be mistaken for neolithic long barrows (but see Llanelwedd, Area 24).

Y Pigwn
RFW pp. 122–5   *828 313* BR

High on top of the dissected escarpment which commands the Tywi valley on the N.W. the Romans twice set up a temporary camp during their early campaigns. The earlier, of 15 ha, and its successor of two-thirds that size, would each have held a whole legion and its attendant auxiliaries. The smaller lies symmetrically askew in the larger, with its S. and W. corners interrupting the earlier banks. 16 of these 'marching camps' are already known in Wales and the Border Country. A simple bank and ditch on the usual rectangular layout, with an additional internal or external bank to protect the entrance gap in each side, was reinforced with a timber fence. The camp might be occupied for only one night, but the defences were quickly erected by the use of every available soldier with the spade and the stake which were part of his standard equipment. The necessary discipline for this activity was achieved at the base forts, where groups of 'practice camps' are a regular feature (see Areas 18, 24, 33, 34).

The mountain ridge of Mynydd-bach Trecastell was the obvious choice for the **Roman road** from Brecon Gaer to the Llandovery fort (Area 36). For about 5 km the present track uses its original *agger*, which is up to 4 m wide. The carefully constructed terraces and zigzags of its descent to the N.W. from Y Pigwn are also easy to follow.

Mynydd-bach Trecastell Circles
SCW p. 135   *833 310* BR

On the same ridge as the Roman camps is a pair of stone circles, a place of religious significance to the people who found good grazing at this height in the more hospitable climate of the Bronze Age. The larger circle of 23 m diameter has just over half of its original 30 stones surviving, none higher than 0.6 m; the low mound at the centre may be sepulchral. Centred 44 m to the S.W. is the small attendant circle of 7.6 m diameter, once consisting of 10 stones, but now reduced to five, rather taller than in the other circle. Four stones once formed an alignment continuing 35 m further to the S.W.

About 5 km to the S. are two more circles by **Nant Tarw** (*819 258*), one of the headwaters of the Usk. Both are on level platforms 110 m apart, just over 19 m in diameter, with about 15 stones surviving of the original 20 or so. A large slab 115 m further to the W. and two small uprights beyond it, are presumably part of the same group, to be compared with the Cerrig Duon site 6 km to the S.S.E. (Area 34). Before visiting two of the good selection of hillforts N. of Brecon, one can get a final taste of the Bronze Age from the remarkable monolith 3.7 m high on a low cairn at **Battle** (*006 306*).

Corn-y-fan Hillfort   *985 354* BR

The escarpment on the S. here served for a large part of the defensive circuit of a small fort with multiple banks round its northern arc. The entrance passage is safely channelled along the steep edge past the bank ends, covered by an extra mound outside.

Pen-y-crug Hillfort
PEW p. 145   *029 303* BR

The three ramparts (four in places) of the fort on this isolated hilltop seem to be all of one period, but the annexe outside the single entrance on the S. may be a remnant of an earlier fort, connecting with an earlier bank curving round the summit inside the main enclosure.

Tŷ Illtud Long Barrow
PCT p. 214   *097 263* BR

One of the only two chambered long cairns of the Usk valley, in an unusual position on the end of a ridge. Like several others it is aligned north–south, and contains a small rectangular chamber with capstone intact, fronted by a rectangular forecourt in the N. end. A series of engravings and inscriptions on the uprights of both parts, including a date variously read as 1312 and 1510, and a symbol interpreted as a harp, have been the subject of argument since the XVII century. They certainly seem to be medieval in character, though no less an authority than the Abbé Breuil considered them prehistoric in origin.

THE MIDDLE USK AND MONNOW   48 km (30 miles)
AREA 28   Brecknock BR, Monmouthshire MM
Map 161; 1″ 141, 142; 2½″ SO *11, 12, 21, 22, 31, 32*

The Usk is deeply confined by mountains before its southward turn to the Severn estuary. Its three main tributaries from the Black Mountains are paralleled by a fourth stream, Afon Honddu, which joins the Monnow to go its separate way down the English border to the Wye at Monmouth. This area of eastern Brecknock and north Monmouthshire is best considered as a unit centred on Abergavenny (there is a small local **museum** in Castle House); or it can be combined with Area 26 or 27. The actual mountain ridges are wild, but the valleys have an attractive lushness that was not missed by early settlers, as already noticed in Area 26. It is great country for energetic recreation, whether on horseback from a pony-trekking centre or on foot from the valley roads, which make the complete mountain passage in two places.

Gwernvale Burial Chamber
PCT p. 214   *211 192* BR
Alongside the main road is a small megalithic chamber, with two slabs converging to form an entrance passage from the W. This is probably the sole surviving element of one of the elaborate long barrows of the region.

Of several Bronze Age standing stones in the valley bottom, the one at **Cwrtygollen** (*232 168*), in full view from the road, is far the most impressive.

Tŷ-isaf Chambered Tomb
Pl. 19; *PCT* p. 213   *182 290* BR
One of the best known of the south Welsh neolithic tombs, owing to its careful excavation in 1938. It also serves as a type site for the whole Black Mountains group of long cairns, which are related to the classic tombs of the Cotswolds. Distinctive features are the placing of the passages to two simple chambers in the sides of the wedge-shaped cairn, and the retention of a forecourt with a blind entrance. A transepted tomb in an oval element in the S. end was also an integral part of the scheme of construction, as shown by the continuity of the double walling. At least 33 individuals were represented by the mass of bones, while associated finds included a good selection of neolithic domestic

Plate 19. Tŷ-isaf Chambered Tomb (Area 28): a typical neolithic round-bottomed bowl, with slightly fluted rim. Scale 1:3. *Photo: National Museum of Wales.*

equipment. In addition to fragmentary flint axes and leaf-shaped arrowheads, the pottery is of great value for comparative purposes in placing the tomb's builders in the main stream of the southern English neolithic rather than that of the Irish Sea area. A cremation burial in a ruinous fourth chamber at the S. end indicated use of the cairn well into Bronze Age times. The **Cwm Fforest Long Cairn** a little further up the stream at *183 294* has dry walling and a capstone, but no signs of upright slabs.

Iron Age hillforts flanking the Black Mountain valleys are not numerous, but show a fair range of adaptation to available sites. **Castell Dinas** (*179 301*) overlooks the top of the pass to Talgarth from a strong position on the isolated end of a spur. The multiple ramparts have an oblique entrance on the N., the cross-bank facing S. is an addition, while a medieval castle was later adapted from the northern enclosure.

Crug Hywel
Pl. 20   *225 206* BR
The end of a ridge descending from a great height in the main core of the Black Mountains was surrounded by a single rampart, ditch and

Plate 20. Crug Hywel (Area 28): a strong system of rampart, ditch and counterscarp bank following the contours of a prominent spur. *Photo: J. K. S. St. Joseph.*

counterscarp bank following the contours in a tear-drop shape. This simple scheme, with an inturned entrance in the curving W. side, was apparently not improved or altered by later users.

Twyn-y-gaer   *294 219* MM

Excavation is gradually sorting out the structural sequence here. The single bank of most of the circuit is doubled at the S. end, with sharply inturned entrances of two separate phases. One cross-bank may even be post-Roman.

Pen-twyn   *321 230* MM

Nearly 3 ha are enclosed by defences of two phases, multiple at the S. end, with an oblique entrance flanked by mounds which suggest some form of guard towers. An internal cross-bank is a later addition.

The Roman names for *Abergavenny* and *Monmouth* are known (Gobannium and Blestium respectively), but no structures are to be seen. The former was apparently a fort, occupied at least until the mid II century, but there was probably no more than a minor civil settlement at Monmouth, where smelting furnaces and pottery of the II and III centuries have been turned up. A small fort at *Pen y Gaer* (*169 219*), controlling the Usk Valley route to Brecon (Fig. 12), seems to have been abandoned in the early II century.

6 SOUTHERN VALLEYS
The Bristol Channel Coast

Figure 23. Pyle (Glam.): a milestone from the Roman road leading south-west from Neath. 'For the Emperor Caesar Marcus Piavonius Victorinus Augustus' (A.D. 268–270). Scale 1:13. *In R.I.S.W. Museum, Swansea (Area 34).*

THE LOWER WYE
AREA 29

53 km (33 miles)
Monmouthshire MM

Map 162, 171; 1″ 155; 2½″ SO *40, 50*, ST *48, 49, 58, 59*

Lying between the lower reaches of two great rivers, the Usk and Wye, south Monmouthshire presents a varied landscape of woods and heavy arable land that was not immediately attractive to early farmers. Neolithic and Bronze Age remains are sparse, but Iron Age settlement was more ambitious. Historically known by their tribal name of Silures, the hillfort dwellers of the I century A.D. were inspired to a final fierce resistance against the Roman conquest under the refugee Belgic prince Caratacus (Caradog), before their eventual pacification and the building of Caerwent as a tribal capital.

Chepstow, an interesting border town near the mouth of the Wye, is at the mercy of modern traffic, so the more secluded Tintern, with its gaunt abbey ruins, is a more attractive proposition as a base for touring this corner of Wales.

Heston Brake Long Cairn
PCT p. 212   *505 886* MM

The present condition of the stone structure and the mound of this chambered long barrow is misleading. Excavation in 1888 showed it to consist of a gallery 8 m long by 1.5 m wide, in the E. end of a barrow 18 m long by 9 m wide. In spite of its position by the Severn, virtually in sight of the Cotswolds, it seems to belong with Gaerllwyd (below) to a tradition of more western origin, distinct from that of the Black Mountains (Areas 26 and 28) and Parc Cwm (Area 35).

Sudbrook Camp
PEW p. 145   *506 874* MM

Just as Sudbrook Point is now the natural site for one end of the Severn

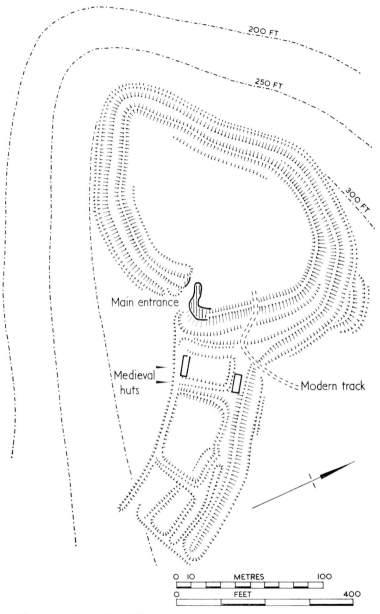

Figure 24. Llanmelin Hillfort (Area 29): a strongly fortified tribal refuge, occupied until the Roman conquest. *After V. E. Nash-Williams.*

railway tunnel, at the most south-westerly constriction of the estuary, so it provided a beach-head for earlier surface crossings. It is not surprising to find an Iron Age strongpoint sited on the promontory to control this route from the mid II century B.C. Excavations in 1934–6 showed that occupation lasted down to the final stand of the Silures against the Romans in the mid I century A.D. Erosion has now reduced the internal area to just over 1 ha.

Llanmelin Hillfort

Fig. 24; *PEW* p. 141   *460 925* MM

Extensively excavated in 1930–32, this hillfort has gained a historical importance that is to be regarded with caution. Its defensive development, from a univallate to a bivallate fort (*c.* 150 B.C.), then to a citadel with strengthened outworks flanking the entrance (50 B.C. onwards), has been coupled with its position overlooking Caerwent to support the idea that it was the tribal capital of the Silures before their subjugation. This role was more probably shared by several forts in the area, each one the individual stronghold of a smaller group, but detailed knowledge of the area is still inadequate.

The so-called 'outpost' at *463 927* has a single rampart, and can be equated with the earliest period of the main fort, though it may not have been so much a strategic outpost as an additional enclosure for the safe keeping of the stock that was part of the agricultural wealth of this particular community.

Caerwent

469 905 MM

The Roman town of Venta Silurum appears to have been founded as the tribal capital of the Silures immediately after the conquest campaign of A.D. 74/5–78, and flourished certainly into the late IV century, perhaps well into the V century. Even though the site was extensively excavated before and after 1900, little is known of its history. The excavations have, however, produced an exceptionally clear plan of the layout of a small Romano-British town of 18 ha. The only surviving remains inside the town walls are those of a few buildings preserved at *Pound Lane*, which itself follows the course of a Roman street. Far more impressive are the *town walls* (which survive to a height of 5.2 m in places), the *S. and E. gates*, and a series of semi-octagonal bastions which were attached to the outer face of the N. and S. walls *c.* A.D. 330–40, All these remains are in State care, and are easily accessible at any time; a guide-book is available.

Finds from the excavation at Caerwent are on view at Newport Museum (described in a special guide), and at the National Museum of Wales. Architectural fragments and two *inscribed stones* are visible within the church at Caerwent. One of these bears the famous 'civitas Silurum' inscription (Frontispiece), from which it can be inferred that a fully civilian regime was established here to satisfy the needs of a vigorous tribe which was dominated by the military superiority of a foreign power.

The pattern of the Roman road system (Fig. 12) is easily seen on the modern map in this coastal strip, the change of direction at *Crick (487 902)* also serving as a junction with the feeder road from the Sudbrook crossing.

Gaerllwyd Burial Chamber
PCT p. 212   *447 968* MM

Though much ruined, and robbed of any mound that may once have covered them, the stones of this tomb show features, such as the two transverse portal stones, which suggest a connection with the megalithic traditions of the Irish Sea rather than those of the Severn-Cotswold culture.

Harold's Stones   *499 051* MM

Though they all now lean in various directions, these three tall stones presumably once stood erect. A Bronze Age date is acceptable, but their purpose remains enigmatic, since their number and their irregular spacing may be only a remnant of a more impressive alignment. Only the middle one seems to have been dressed, and has two cupmarks on its S. side.

Although the river is an obvious natural frontier, and today forms the boundary between Wales and England, it is interesting to note that the VIII century Mercian frontier work *Offa's Dyke* followed the top of the eastern escarpment, leaving unrestricted use of the river to the Welsh as far N. as Redbrook *(54 10)*.

The Bulwarks   *538 927* MM

Sited with a commanding view over the Severn estuary, on a cliff which reduces the length of artificial defence needed, this presumably pre-Roman fort is really no larger than a homestead enclosure, but was strongly protected by two banks facing the level ground on the W. It is in State care, open always without charge.

THE LOWER USK   19 km (12 miles)
AREA 30   Monmouthshire MM
               Map 171; 1″ 154, 155; 2½″ ST *28, 29, 38, 39*

Newport is both the commercial and cultural focus of south Monmouthshire, and will provide all the needs of the archaeological tourist, including a fine new museum. Raglan and Usk have hotels in charming
settings; though at a distance from the chief sites, they would serve for a
combined tour of Areas 29 and 30.

   The terrain flanking the lower reaches of the Usk has much the same
character as Area 29, though there is a steeper rise on the W. to the
coal-bearing uplands. The archaeological variety is similar, dominated
by Iron Age fortified settlements which fell into disuse with the Roman
occupation, this time more directly under the military influence of the
great legionary fortress at Caerleon.

Tredegar Camp   *289 868* MM

On the outskirts of Newport, in parkland behind a housing estate. The
medieval ring motte inside has its own subrectangular bailey, all
enclosed by the multiple ramparts of the Iron Age fort, widespread on
the S. and probably of two periods.

   Remote but accessible on a broad spur of the mountain fringe is
Twmbarlwm (*243 926*), a single-ramparted contour fort apparently
unfinished, with two large gaps in its circuit. The medieval castle mound
at its E. end may have been so sited to take advantage of the earlier
work for a ready-made bailey.

Lodge Wood Camp   *323 913* MM

One may suppose that this two-period fort on an isolated ridge overlooking Caerleon effectively controlled the lowest crossing of the Usk
in its day, as the Roman fort did later. First a single bank with a simple
entrance enclosed less than 0.5 ha in a narrow ellipse, but the defences
were later elaborated, with an oblique entrance, around an area about
seven times the size.

Caerleon
Pl. 21, Fig. 12; *RFW* p. 29   *340 907* MM
The village of Caerleon, on the northern outskirts of Newport, occupies

Plate 21. Caerleon (Area 30): aerial view of the Roman fortress from the west, with the amphitheatre in the foreground. *Photo: H. Tempest, for Nat. Mus. Wales.*

the site of Roman Isca, the fortress of the Second Augustan Legion. The defences enclose an area of about 21 ha, sufficient to accommodate the 5,000–6,000 legionaries. The fortress was founded *c.* A.D. 74–5 after the conquest of south Wales, and was intensively occupied until about 120. Thereafter the occupation was on a much reduced scale, since the bulk of the Legion was on active service in northern Britain. The II century saw the refurbishing of the earthen defences with a stone wall, stone-built gates, towers and internal buildings. Effective military occupation ended perhaps in the mid IV century.

The *fortress defences* are best seen on the S. and the remains of *barrack blocks*, interval towers and other structures can be viewed at any time within the S.W. angle. The well-preserved remains of an *amphitheatre* and of a small *bath building* outside the S.E. wall are also in State care, to be viewed in standard hours; a guide-book is available. A large civil settlement lay to the S. of the fortress, and temples to Diana and Mithras are known to exist somewhere in this area. A small *museum* at Caerleon houses many of the most important discoveries. The remainder of the finds are in the National Museum of Wales, where an excellent guide-book can be purchased.

The only other important military site of this area was the fort of Burrium at *Usk* (*379 007*). The current series of excavations have already shown that the primary purpose was as a base fortress for early campaigning, before the more permanent fortress of Caerleon was established. An extensive series of granaries and workshops has been revealed in the low-lying area near the prison, where flooding must have been an additional inducement for the move. Occupation of the site in the II and III centuries seems to have been entirely civil.

Newport Museum
Dock St.   *312 879* MM

The municipal arts centre is now splendidly housed in a new complex of buildings, in which the museum collections have been well treated. Prehistoric material is limited to discoveries of local significance, whereas most of the display cases are devoted to the comprehensive discoveries from the excavations at Caerwent (Area 29). A good look at the civil and domestic objects here is essential for a full understanding of provincial urban life under the Romans.

VALE OF GLAMORGAN EAST   63 km (39 miles)
AREA 31   Glamorgan GL
Map 170, 171; 1″ 154; 2½″ ST *06–08, 17, 18*

West of Cardiff and south of the coal-bearing mountains, the land descends in a series of broad shelves to the sea. Favourable soil and climate have extended a steady invitation through post-glacial times to settlers coming variously up the western seaways from foreign parts or expanding across the Bristol Channel from earlier homes in southern England. The Channel itself would have been as much a unifying element for the former as it was a barrier for the latter. E. of Cowbridge the intake of arable land was delayed until final Iron Age and Roman times, when the heavier plough was introduced, but neolithic burial chambers are evidence of an early beginning on lighter soil areas.

Cardiff, with its castle built on Roman foundations, and the National Museum of Wales, deserves a whole day to itself. Those who prefer a base outside the capital city may be disappointed with the choice of accommodation elsewhere.

The National Museum of Wales   *183 769* GL

The museum forms the eastern end of the fine façade of civic buildings in Cathays Park; the archaeological collections, based on the former Cardiff Municipal Museum in 1912 and built up first by John Ward, then by Sir Mortimer Wheeler from 1920, were set up in the present building in 1924. A recent extension to the N.W. has been largely necessitated by continued expansion in archaeology under the late Sir Cyril Fox and Dr. V. E. Nash-Williams, followed by W. F. Grimes and H. N. Savory. The museum publication, *The Prehistory of Wales*, serves as a guide to the prehistoric collections, and equally good guides to other periods and special collections make detailed information unnecessary here. Notable exhibits include the Iron Age find from Llyn Cerrig Bach (Area 1) and many originals and replicas of inscribed and decorated stones, both Christian and pagan; outstanding among the latter is the meandering spiral brought on its stone from Bryn Celli Ddu (Fig. 5). Among latter-day relics it is worth noting the insignia of the Gorsedd of Bards, specially devised for the dignity of that body. To complete the picture of these modern Druids, there is a stone circle in the garden in front of the museum, erected when Cardiff took its turn as host for the National Eisteddfod. Access at the time of writing, free; the hours of opening are those normal to a State museum, including Sunday afternoons.

The **Welsh Folk Museum** at St. Fagans Castle (*120 772*) also deserves a special visit. Though it contains few actual objects of pre-Norman date, it is devoted to just those traditional aspects of Welsh culture which have their Celtic roots in the Iron Age, and which have survived in turn both Roman uniformity and English legal oppression. The generous gift of the castle and grounds by the Earl of Plymouth in 1946 began the separate existence of the museum after twenty years as a department of the National Museum, inspired throughout by the breadth of vision of its Curator, Iorwerth Peate. The open-air museum idea, in which whole domestic and industrial units are reconstructed, had been pioneered in Scandinavia in the 1890s.

Cardiff Roman Fort

RFW p. 70; *INV* No. 736   *181 766* GL

For a considerable part of the circuit of the walls of the medieval castle, the lowest courses exactly follow the ramparts of a Roman fort; the upper parts of them are XIX century restoration by Lord Bute. To see any of the original Roman stonework, access must be obtained to the basement in the S. wall, unfortunately not normally granted to the casual enquirer. The E. side and the N. gate have been restored to a fair likeness of the Roman original. Probably built on the site of a I century fort of which no trace remains, this stone fort was an attempt to provide defence against sea raiders around A.D. 400.

The civil life of the countryside W. of Cardiff under the Romans has to be deduced from chance finds. Two villa sites of contrasting character have been extensively excavated. At *Ely* (*147 762*) the establishment was apparently concerned with an iron smelting and foundry business during the two centuries that cover its three main building phases from *c.* 125. At *Whitton* (*081 713*) a recent series of excavations has revealed a flourishing farm of the typical Roman pattern, the direct successor of a late Iron Age settlement with exceptionally well-built round huts.

Caerau Hillfort, Ely

Fig. 25; *INV* No. 673   *134 750* GL

A triangular area of about 5 ha forming a natural plateau has been

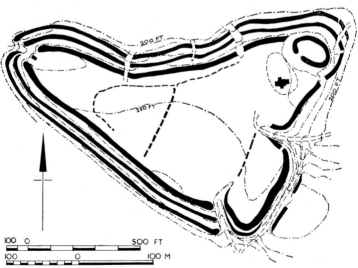

Figure 25. Caerau Hillfort, Ely (Area 31): three ramparts surround a natural plateau to form one of the strongest forts of South Wales. *After R.C.A.M., Crown Copyright.*

fortified with three ramparts on its N. and S. sides. On the E. these are reduced to one massive bank and ditch commanding the only level ground outside. An eastern entrance is occupied by the modern road, and is not easy to make out, but one at the southern corner is clearer. Pre-Roman and Romano-British pottery have been picked up, and occupation probably continued from then onward, for a medieval ringwork stands in the N.E. corner, and the church may also indicate a village settlement.

In contrast with Caerau, the strongly fortified site at **Dinas Powis** (*148 723*) was not defended until the V century A.D., though there was some occupation in the pre-Roman Iron Age. The multiple defences now visible all belong to the XI to XIII centuries.

St. Lythans Chambered Cairn

INV No. 42   *101 723* GL

The conspicuously gaunt skeleton of the burial chamber here has inspired many early antiquarians to Druidic interpretations, but it must be seen with the worn-down remains of a long cairn as another

Plate 22. Tinkinswood Chambered Cairn (Area 31): the low entry from forecourt to chamber. Scale in feet. *Photo: R.C.A.M., Crown Copyright.*

K

specimen of the south Welsh megalithic tombs of which Tinkinswood (below) is the prime example. It is in State care, open always without charge. A pamphlet is available.

Tinkinswood Chambered Cairn

Pl. 22; *INV* No. 40   *092 733* GL

John Ward's excavations here in 1914 were outstanding for their time, and the careful restoration does justice to the importance of the monument. The enormous capstone, estimated to weigh 40 tons, was locally quarried along with its supporting slabs, to form a simple end chamber in a dry-walled cairn of the typical Severn-Cotswold wedge-shaped form. The back of the funnel-shaped forecourt was walled to the chamber roof, leaving only a low entrance gap at one corner. At least 50 individuals were represented by the mass of bones recovered, along with several fragments of plain pottery and Beaker ware. A slab-lined pit in the body of the mound was not part of the original layout, but internal lines of upright stones are either ritual in purpose, or a practical demarcation of family shares in the building of a communal tomb. In State care, open always without charge; a pamphlet is available (see p. 195) describing this and the St. Lythans tomb together.

Settlements of the Neolithic period are usually found only by chance, as happened when a Bronze Age cairn was completely excavated at *Sant-y-nyll* (*101 783*) in 1958. An oval ring of post-holes 4.6 m by 3.7 m across represented a hut succeeding two smaller ones, amid domestic refuse which indicated a sheep-farming economy. Pottery was of late neolithic type distinct from that of the long cairns, and probably represented a phase of peasant life transitional to the Bronze Age proper.

Another burial chamber at **Cae'r-arfau** (*077 821*) is easy to visit at the side of an abandoned lane, but is a simple remnant that defies interpretation in the absence of any traces of a cairn.

VALE OF GLAMORGAN WEST   80 km (50 miles)
AREA 32   Glamorgan GL
                             Map 170; 1″ 153, 154; 2½″ ss *87, 88, 96–99*

West of Bridgend the Vale narrows to extinction amid the smoke of the steel furnaces of Port Talbot. The lower land S. of the main road and rail routes is on well-drained limestone, desirable terrain for primitive settlement that involved tillage. For shepherds and herdsmen of the later Iron Age the broad hill centred on Mynydd Margam provided good pasturage, based on distinctive embanked refuges which often lacked the advantage of naturally steep slopes, but were themselves built on slopes in comparatively vulnerable positions. A topographical feature of the coastline is the succession of sand-dune areas, which made their major encroachment in medieval times. Merthyr Mawr Warren has been particularly productive of finds of all periods, Kenfig Burrows conceal a medieval town, while Margam Burrows, now suffering from urban expansion, could have been the location of early monastic settlement.

For accommodation Bridgend and Porthcawl offer the hotels appropriate to market town and fun resort respectively. For motoring antiquarians the Southerndown-Ogmore hotel circuit will be more appealing.

Caer Dynnaf
INV No. 670   *983 742* GL
Though there has been considerable ploughing and adaptation of the defences into field boundaries, two ramparts can be made out on the N. and E. of this major hillfort, and three lines on the S. and W. The complicated entrance at the W. end is probably the result of development through more than one phase. The low banks and hollows in the enclosure may all belong to a late agricultural occupation, for Roman pottery of III and IV century date has been found in trial excavations.

A long history of farming on the classic Roman pattern was revealed in the full excavation of a villa near *Llantwit Major* (*959 700*). The layout consisted of a double courtyard, on two sides of which were the main domestic buildings, including a full suite of baths, all constructed *c.* 150. There were extensive barns and workshops of several periods, and there was a major phase of rebuilding in stone *c.* 300, embellished with some fine mosaic floors and painted plaster. One wing of the villa contained the disorderly remains of men and horses apparently massacred *c.* 350, after which it is doubtful whether the establishment was fully revived, though the later insertion of some proper Christian burials has been taken to suggest that this was the V century home of St. Illtud, the patron of Llantwit Major. There are some fine **decorated memorial stones** at the church (*966 687*), including one to an VIII century Samson, probably an abbot who had adopted the name of the

V century Samson, who in turn was a product of the Celtic monastery along with his more famous compatriot St. David. The present double church, though of great interest in itself, contains no trace of any earlier monastic remains.

On the headland beyond the village **Castle Ditches** (*960 674*) is a well-sited Iron Age promontory fort, though the triple defences across the landward plateau are too overgrown for full appreciation of their effectiveness.

Nash Point Promontory Fort
INV No. 667   *915 685* GL

The striking succession of four ramparts, with flat-bottomed ditches between, gave a defensive depth of 60 m to what was probably once a fair-sized headland, rather like Castle Ditches above. Erosion has now reduced the interior almost to nothing, but the strategic layout of the entrance is clear, diverting all comers through the steep landward cwm to a final terraced trackway below the innermost rampart. A single medieval 'pillow mound' (artificial rabbit warren) is the only internal feature.

Dunraven Promontory Fort
INV No. 666   *887 728* GL

The fort occupies a headland well separated from the hinterland by a steep scarp, used to advantage first by the Iron Age inhabitants, and finally by the builders of the now demolished Dunraven Castle. The W. side is badly eroded by the sea, which has reduced the defended area from about 10 to 6.5 ha, probably taking with it the whole of a main entrance through the twin ramparts. There may also have been a rampart facing S. near the summit, leaving a low-lying spit of land undefended, within which is a good group of **'pillow mounds'** (see Llanelwedd, Area 24). On the gentle slope, N. of the summit are more of these mounds, and a group of ten platforms and hollows, which may be the sites of Iron Age dwellings.

Ty-du Standing Stone
INV No. 555   *802 837* GL

Not far from the road is a fine specimen of what was with little doubt a Bronze Age burial marker, a monolith of rectangular section, 1.5 m by 0.9 m along its faces, and 2.5 m high.

Margam Abbey Museum of Stones

INV Nos. 846 etc.; *ECMW*   *800 864* GL

In the old school close to Margam Abbey is an important collection of inscribed and ornamented stones, in State care, and accessible for a small admission charge on Wed., Sat. and Sun. afternoons. Descriptive leaflets are available, but the more outstanding stones include Roman-style inscriptions of the VI century, and IX–XI century inscriptions in Hiberno-Saxon lettering on stones incorporating crosses and elaborate interlaced decoration, the finest stone of all being the Great Cross of Conbelin, sadly lacking part of its shaft and damaged on one face. The inscription is brief and oddly placed, but the decoration includes a delightful hunting scene of two horsemen following two dogs which are pulling down a stag. The two figures on the front are of the Virgin and St. John, in a style familiar in Irish manuscripts.

The course of the Roman road from Pyle to Neath is well attested by no less than five milestones found in a distance of 17 km (one is seen in Fig. 23). All bear inscriptions which date them within the bracket A.D. 258–324.

Mynydd-y-castell

INV No. 613   *806 866* GL

There is a single rampart, best preserved on the E. side of this isolated summit, reaching an external height of 8.5 m at one point. A counter-scarp bank is eroded into the form of a shelf for much of the circuit. From a point in the E. side a trace of an earlier, perhaps unfinished, rampart turns inward, to end with a further inturn as for a gateway. The surviving entrance at the S.W. ascends a ramp leading to a natural hollow; another at the N.E. has been confused by quarrying.

Y Bwlwarcau

Pl. 23; *INV* No. 693   *839 885* GL

When bracken growth allows, the complicated layout here can be seen to consist of a pentagonal enclosure of 0.3 ha with a substantial bank, superimposed on an earlier one of twice the size. The earlier one had a double-banked outer enclosure of about 4.4 ha, perhaps more of a boundary than a defensive work. There are further enclosures using parts of these banks, but all seem to have originated in a complicated history of agricultural use, which is the underlying reason for the choice of an open slope rather than a naturally defensible hilltop.

Twmpath Diwlith (*832 888*) is one of a group of good Bronze Age barrows in an area now actively afforested, so that their location is

Plate 23. Y Bwlwarcau (Area 32): the wide-spaced defences on a broad slope distinguish this farm settlement from the strong tribal refuge. *Photo: J. K. S. St. Joseph.*

often difficult. Here too, by the roadside, is a replica of the *Bodvoc Stone (831 888)* at its original site in a Bronze Age ring cairn. The true stone is in Margam Museum (above). The Bronze Age cairns of the Vale of Glamorgan are mostly in cultivated land, and thus not easily accessible. In addition, many of the best known sites have been swept away in development projects, of which the most destructive was the creation of wartime airfields, with agricultural improvement as a close second. Fortunately the harvest of archaeological detail from the necessary rescue excavations has been a rich one, revealing a wide range of constructional and ritual detail for the whole range of the Early and Middle Bronze Age. The late Sir Cyril Fox published his own illuminating contribution in *Life and Death in the Bronze Age* (1959), based on seven sites in this area, and there are equally careful records of half a dozen others. For example the *Pond Cairn* at Coity (*915 812*) showed a complicated sequence of construction, beginning with an adult cremation in an overhanging-rim urn under a heap of stones. Both this and a dedicatory child-burial were covered by a turf stack, enclosed in turn by a stone wall. After various rituals, which involved the digging of a pit and the scattering of charcoal and grain, the whole was covered with a stone cairn 19 m in diameter.

THE EASTERN COAL VALLEYS   71 km (44 miles)
AREA 33   Glamorgan GL
Map 160, 170, 171; 1″ 154; 2½″ SN *90*, SO *00, 10*, SS *99*, ST *09, 19*

In this battle-scarred area of iron and coal exploitation, suitably commemorated in *Cyfarthfa Castle Museum* (*042 073*), the touring holiday-maker is not expected to spend much time, so accommodation tends to be of the simple kind, apart from hotels in Aberdare, which is central enough. The mountain crossings are by well-engineered roads, largely built with cheap labour in years of depression, and will give splendid views in between visits to the somewhat scattered archaeological sites. The ridges had a changing significance in successive periods of the past, from peaceful Bronze Age and Iron Age pasturing to Roman military movement and campaign.

At the edge of this area, on one of the highest summits of the county, is **Crug yr Afan** (*920 954*), a remarkable burial mound consisting of a stone cairn 10 m across, set on a flat-topped mound of twice that diameter, surrounded in turn by a flat berm and ditch. There was formerly a setting of upright stones round the cairn, in which a burial cist was found in 1902. The most remarkable find was a small bone dagger, grooved along the edges in a form familiar in the Early Bronze Age of Wessex, and thus consistent with the bell-barrow form of the mound.

An oval stone embanked ring, **Pebyll** (*910 972*), within reach to the N.W., is one of those Bronze Age sites for which it is difficult to choose between a burial and a ritual function. The interior space of 25 m by 23 m seems to have been levelled slightly, and there are two entrances, which would not be expected in a ring cairn.

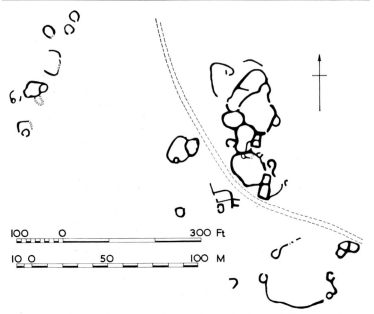

Figure 26. Garreg Lwyd Hut Group (Area 33): the undefended settlement of Iron Age pastoralists. *After R.C.A.M., Crown Copyright.*

Garreg Lwyd Hut Group
Fig. 26; *INV* No. 711   *932 019* GL
Above a steep drop to the S.W. are two groups of irregular enclosures built of the abundant loose scree to be found here. The walling is a metre high in places, faced with orthostats or dry-laid, and the E. group has a dozen round huts of about 3 m diameter incorporated in the layout. The whole site was completely undefended, and presumably the settlement of mountain-top shepherds of the Iron Age, distinguishable from the lowland cultivators and hillfort builders as the direct inheritors of a Bronze Age way of life. Excavations in 1921 produced leather and the by-products of iron working.

Running up the W. side of the stream beyond this settlement and ending at the steep cliff above Llyn Fawr is **Ffos Toncenglau** (*919 020* to *917 030*), a stone-faced boundary bank of about the IX century A.D. The intention seems to have been to channel movement along the ridge route known as *Cefn Ffordd*, with perhaps more political than military effect.

Plate 24. Llyn Fawr (Area 33): one of two bronze cauldrons from the Iron Age hoard discovered in the lake. Scale 1:6. *Photo: National Museum of Wales.*

From *Llyn Fawr* itself (*917 035*) came a remarkable collection of metalwork when the lake was adapted as a reservoir. Of the 24 objects, most were of bronze, including two cauldrons (Plate 24) and an axe of Irish type, a razor and decorative objects of continental origin, and two sickles. A third sickle had been copied in iron, while a spearhead and a sword of continental type, also of iron, combine to give the assemblage a date of *c.* 600 B.C. The circumstances of the find are harder to explain, but are more likely to indicate deliberate deposit, for later recovery or as a votive offering, than casual accumulation from a lake-side settlement in such a sunless spot.

Carn Bugail
INV No. 156   *100 036* GL
On a broad summit is the ruin of a cairn in which its early excavator recorded three parallel burial cists 3 m long, thus probably for inhumation rather than cremation. Only one of these is detectable now, but the substantial kerb of 16 m diameter is still visible.

The ridge of Gelligaer Common and Mynydd Eglwysilan further south were chosen by the Romans as the main access route from the mountains towards the coast at Cardiff (Fig. 12). The forts at *Merthyr Tydfil (050 068)* and *Caerphilly (154 873)* served as control points at either end of this route, but cannot be easily appreciated on the ground. The broad southern part of the common around Gelligaer appears to have been an important centre of military activity based on the fort there, including the building of a **practice camp** at *131 991* and of two at *138 992*. The *road* itself is not clearly distinguishable from the modern road which follows it, until the latter diverges from it in passing Carn Bugail (above). **Clawdd Trawscae** is a cross-ridge dyke clearly created at a later date to control movement along the established route, which it crossed at *117 002*.

Gelligaer Roman Fort
RFW p. 88; *INV* No. 738   *134 971* GL

The rectangular earthworks here are reasonably well preserved, and consist of an earlier earth-and-timber fort of 2.2 ha on the N.W., regarded as a late I century site, abandoned in favour of a new stone fort on the S.E. in the early II century. The latter is a square of 1.4 ha, with four gateways; four angle towers and eight intermediate turrets were added, as was an annexe of 0.75 ha on the S.E. The internal stone buildings were of as fine a quality as any in south Wales, clearly indicating the permanent role of the garrison, which was maintained more or less continuously in some form until the IV century. John Ward's timely intervention in a local society's excavation campaign at the beginning of the present century has made this one of the best documented examples of a Roman frontier fort; outstanding are the regimental baths in the annexe, which had some rooms finely decorated with painted plaster. The whole site is well represented in displays in the National Museum in Cardiff.

Maen Catwg
INV No. 49   *127 974* GL

An isolated block of stone bears a random series of 50 cupmarks up to 115 mm in diameter and 60 mm deep, of which some are nearly weathered away. Such groups, rare in Wales, are generally regarded as Bronze Age in origin, though they occur on the capstones of neolithic cromlechs at Trelyffant (Area 41) and Bachwen (Area 5).

THE WESTERN COAL VALLEYS
AREA 34

110 km (68 miles)

Brecknock BR, Glamorgan GL

Map 159, 160, 170; 1″ 140, 153; 2½″ SN 60, 70, 80–82, SS 69, 79

The topography of the western coalfield owes its different character to the formation of the Swansea and Neath Valleys along lines of weakness in the ancient geological structure, diverting in a south-westerly direction a large share of the southward drainage of Fforest Fawr. Natural conditions do not seem to have encouraged early farming settlement, so that archaeological sites are limited to a scatter of Bronze Age burial and ritual monuments, as well as the roads and control points of the Roman period. Neath is well placed for the northward journeys of this area, but Swansea or the holiday complex of south-east Gower may be preferred as a base for taking in Area 35 at the same time.

Swansea Museum

Victoria Rd.   659 927 GL

The Royal Institution of South Wales has stood since 1838 as a symbol of culture on the edge of Swansea's dock area. The Institution's interest has persisted mainly in natural history and later local history, while the archaeological collection has tended to be augmented on a chance basis. There is a notable display of finds from excavations in Minchin Hole (Area 35), covering Iron Age and Dark Age occupations; the Roman forts at Neath, Coelbren and Loughor are well represented, and there is also some good Bronze Age pottery from early and recent excavations. In the entrance hall is a Roman milestone from Pyle (827 822; Fig. 23). A Roman altar from Loughor has an ogam inscription added on one corner, an early VI century Latin stone commemorates Macaritinus, son of Bericius, and two IX–X century cross-shafts have ecclesiastical figures carved in low relief. The Museum is open from 10.00 to 17.00, Monday to Saturday, for a small charge.

Roman Practice Camps, Gorseinon

Pl. 25; *INV* Nos. 744–5; *RFW* pp. 126–9   609 972 GL

On the broad low ridge of Mynydd Carn-goch are two easily accessible specimens about 25 m square, built presumably by troops on exercise from the fort recently identified at *Loughor* (*563 979*) beneath the medieval castle there.

Carn Goch itself (*605 981*), one of the largest Bronze Age burial

Plate 25. Gorseinon (Area 34): practice camps constructed by Roman troops on field exercises. *Photo: J. K. S. St. Joseph.*

mounds in Glamorgan, was thoroughly mutilated in the XIX century in the name of discovery. A stone ring beneath an earth covering had been robbed of its primary burial, but there were at least nine secondary cremations with urns (some are in Swansea Museum).

Carn Llechart

INV No. 66   *697 063* GL

One of the finest Bronze Age burial sites in Glamorgan, with an unusual circle of contiguous slabs set up round a large rectangular cist. The slabs were obtained from rock outcrops at the edge of the ridge close by. Just below the brow, S.W. of the circle at *696 062*, some large slabs are associated with smaller uprights in a way that suggests a much ruined **megalithic tomb**, though experts differ over its interpretation.

Cerrig Duon Circle

Fig. 27; *SCW* p. 138   *852 206* BR

On the W. of the Tawe near its source, on a shelf projecting from the hillside, is a fairly regular circle of 20 stones, with possibly 8 missing. None is over half a metre high, but they are more prominent than the

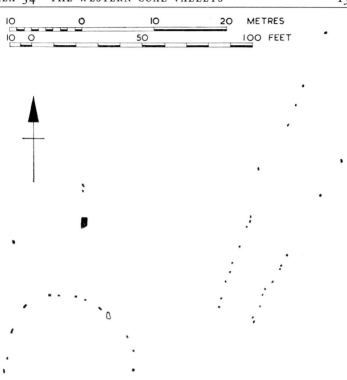

Figure 27. Cerrig Duon (Area 34): a stone circle and alignment of the Bronze Age. *After W. F. Grimes.*

two almost parallel lines N.E. of the circle, which must be in a significant association with it, as well as with the 1.8 m high Maen Mawr on the N.

Alignments are not common in Wales, so the six stones of **Saeth Maen** (*833 154*) are worth the climb from Craig y Nos. Here too the western slopes of the valley contain the well-explored and advertised caves of Dan-yr-ogof, famous for their natural formations. Less well known are the archaeological discoveries of a small excavation in *Ogof yr Esgyrn* (*839 160*), which included some Middle Bronze Age

burial pottery, though the main use of the cave was for habitation in the
II and IV centuries A.D.

Coelbren Roman Fort

Fig. 12; *INV* No. 731; *RFW* p. 81   *859 107* GL

One of the smaller forts of the system, for 500 cavalry or 1000 infantry,
a comparatively unaltered specimen of late I century earth-and-timber
construction, abandoned *c.* 140. The finds of the 1904 excavations are
at Swansea Museum. There was some sort of annexe on the N.E. side,
through which a **road** can be traced descending to a stream crossing
before setting course for Brecon. A particularly well preserved stretch
between ditches 6 m apart can be reached from *873 114*.

South-westward the route lies along the Hirfynydd ridge, a satisfying
walk over moorland and through forest plantations, passing first at
828 066 an earthwork 20 m square explained as a *signal station*; then at
823 058 a mound with a square hollow which may be the site of a
milestone; and finally an incomplete *signal station* at *812 040*.

Blaen-cwm-bach Marching Camp

INV No. 740; *RFW* p. 124   *796 987* GL

On the ridge S.E. of the Neath Valley the W. end of this 27 ha camp is
easily located where the road passes into it to the N. of an original
entrance. The elongated shape (908 m by 295 m) takes advantage of the
form of the ground, using a marshy patch below a steep scarp for the
W. half of the N. side.

Neath Roman Fort

INV No. 734; *RFW* p. 98   *748 977* GL

The lie of the fort of Nidum has been well established, half on each side
of the main road. Excavations where possible have found evidence of an
original timber fort of *c.* A.D. 75, superseded in stone in 120 for a dura-
tion of perhaps as little as 10 years. Parts of the S.E. and S. gateways are
in State guardianship, open to view in the housing estate.

Carreg Hir

INV No. 554   *744 953* GL

Set up in the playground of Cwrt Sart School, just visible from the
gate in Old Road when the school is closed, this standing stone presumably marked a Bronze Age burial before it was re-sited. It is 2.7 m
high.

THE GOWER PENINSULA

AREA 35

82 km (51 miles)

Glamorgan GL

Map 159; 1″ 152, 153; 2½″ SS *48, 49, 58, 59*

The peninsula has become the playground of Swansea and its industrial neighbours, as well as being an area of natural beauty sought after by visitors from afar. Its comparative peace and freedom from offensive development are due to early planning and control, and to the efforts of the Gower Society, The National Trust and other interested bodies. Access to the cliffs and beaches is not easy for the motorist, who is advised to take to his feet if in doubt. The bays of the S.E. corner of the peninsula provide a variety of lodgings, as do such places as Port Eynon, Rhosili and Reynoldston.

In Swansea Museum (Area 34) are many of the discoveries from a wide range of burial and settlement sites in Gower, including some justly famous caves in the limestone cliffs of the south coast. *Minchin Hole (555 868)* is the only coastal cave which can still be seen in the same relationship to the sea as it had at the time of occupation (from the pre-Roman Iron Age to the VII century A.D. in this case). Those which have yielded Stone Age material looked out over a considerable plain when the sea level was lower in pleistocene times. *Bacon Hole (560 868)* in the same cliffs at Pennard was famous for a while in 1912, until the red streaks on its walls faded away and showed the Abbé Breuil, in spite of his sound judgement in such matters, to have been mistaken in pronouncing them to be of Stone Age origin. This may well be a natural phenomenon which appears intermittently, but the explanation which gained favour at the time was that a member of a salvage crew sheltering there a few years earlier had cleaned a red paint brush on the cave wall.

High Pennard Promontory Fort

INV No. 702   *567 866* GL

Cliffs on the S. and W. made artificial protection unnecessary there, but two ramparts and ditches cross the landward area, where intervening crags complicate the defensive effect. Excavations in 1940 revealed details of construction, including a timber gateway and a guard hut. The occupation was dated to the I and II centuries A.D., though it may be doubted whether the Romans would have allowed the defences to be maintained after their rule began *c.* 80.

Cat Hole Cave

INV No. 17   *538 900* GL

High in the side of a wooded valley, facing W., this was probably a
reasonably comfortable habitation towards the end of glacial times.
The flint industry recovered here shows the occupants to have belonged
to the British variant of the Upper Palaeolithic known as Creswellian
from its type site in Derbyshire.

Parc Cwm Long Cairn

Fig. 28; *INV* No. 36   *537 898* GL

First excavated in 1869, but fully examined and conserved in 1960–1,
this is a fine specimen of chambered tomb, which presents most of the
classic features of the Severn-Cotswold Group of the Neolithic period.
The wedge-shaped cairn with bell-shaped forecourt was neatly revetted
with local stone, around a central gallery with four side chambers.
Some 24 individuals were represented by the bones recovered, most of
which had been successively disturbed by later burials, for this was a
communal tomb for continuing use by the local group who built it. The

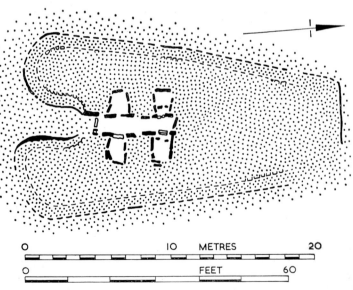

Figure 28. Parc Cwm Long Cairn (Area 35): a classic Severn-Cotswold tomb.
After R. J. C. Atkinson.

plan is a much more unitary conception than many others of this period. In State care, accessible at any time without charge.

On **Penmaen Burrows** (*531 881*) are the remains of the chambers of what was in all probability a very similar tomb, but sand has obscured what may have survived of the surrounding cairn.

The Knave Cliff Fort
INV No. 699   *432 864* GL
Not a typical promontory fort, as the ramparts are long in relation to the depth of the defended area of only about 0.1 ha. Two banks and ditches form about a third of a circle from cliff to cliff, with entrances towards the W., taking advantage of the lie of outcrops. Excavation in 1938 showed extensive use of large limestone blocks in the ramparts, and produced pottery of pre-Roman date comparable with that from the well-known Glastonbury 'lake-dwellings'. There was no evidence of continuing habitation after the Roman conquest.

Not far along the coast to the S.E. is the Goat's Hole at *Paviland* (*437 858*), the cave in which William Buckland in 1823 found the famous 'Red Lady', buried with a number of ivory ornaments in a deposit of cave earth strongly impregnated with iron oxide. The 'lady' was transferred to the University Museum at Oxford, and is now known to have been a well-built man of about 25 years, assigned to the Crô-Magnon race of the French Upper Palaeolithic, and even dated by radiocarbon to about 16,500 B.C. He is probably to be equated with a flint industry of 'final Aurignacian' character, but still a few thousand years prior to the Creswellian of Cat Hole. The cave is not easily accessible on the rocky shore, but high on a grassy cliff-top further S.E. is the small entrance of *Long Hole* (*452 851*), where in 1861 (just after the publication of Darwin's *Origin of Species*) flint implements were recognised in direct association with the bones of extinct fauna, formerly classed as 'antediluvian'.

Thurba Head Fort
INV No. 698   *422 871* GL
The craggy shape of this promontory led to some ingenious siting of the defences to cut off unwanted approach from the flanks, and the main entrance was channelled below a high cliff on the S.E., rather than through the ramparts on the saddle above. There seem to have been two phases of building, first a stone wall curving between the cliffs, and now much robbed, followed by a system of two banks further to the N.E., but neither dated by excavation.

L

Hardings Down West Fort

INV No. 687   *434 908* GL

Sited rather weakly on a sloping spur of Hardings Down, this is one of a group of three of varying character. Excavation in 1962 revealed a stone-revetted bank inside a V-shaped ditch, a gateway of four large posts, and a round house of 10 m diameter in the interior, where plain Iron Age B pottery gave a probable pre-Roman date. Two slight ramparts on the E. can only be seen as part of some unfinished additional defence.

In view from Hardings Down are the two ruined megalithic tombs known as the **Sweyne's Howes** (or Swine Houses, less correctly) at *421 898*, sited 100 m apart at the foot of the main eastern scarp of Rhosili Down. The form of their chambers cannot be fully made out, but the interest lies in the nearly circular shape of their cairns, which puts them outside the Severn-Cotswold tradition of S.E. Wales.

From here the tidal island of **Burry Holms** invites a visit. A promontory fort (*398 926*), formed by a single rampart with a simple entrance gap defending the W. end of the island, is dated to the Roman period by pottery. The *ecclesiastical settlement* (*401 926*) on the low eastern end of the island began with a timber church in a stone-walled enclosure like an Irish cashel. All the visible remains, including the church which developed from apsidal to rectangular form, are XII century or later.

Llanmadoc Bulwark

INV No. 689   *443 927* GL

The complicated layout incorporates remains of at least two periods, not easy to disentangle but probably univallate at first, followed by a scheme of multiple ramparts which made partial use of the earlier circuit. There is a close sequence of four banks and ditches across the ridge to the W., and a widely spaced system flanking the direct entrance way on the E.

Cil Ifor Top Hillfort

INV No. 665   *505 923* GL

A classic multivallate fort as it now appears, perhaps succeeding an earlier single circuit. The close-set defences make intelligent use of the shape of the hill, especially in the zigzag form of the entrance arrangements on the S.W. The N.E. end contains a ringwork probably of medieval date.

Plate 26. Arthur's Stone (Area 35): an erratic boulder with a burial chamber formed beneath it. *Photo: R.C.A.M., Crown Copyright.*

Arthur's Stone (Maen Ceti)

Pl. 26; *INV* No. 33   *491 905* GL

A huge glacial boulder has been underpinned with uprights, of which nine remain, to form two irregular burial compartments beneath. The surrounding circular bank is the direct result of the construction process, rather than a deliberately chosen cairn form. Indeed, it may never have been finished, if the large slice of the boulder lying on the W. side split off at that time. All kinds of legends and literary references surround this landmark, including the recurrent idea of a pebble flung by a giant—in this case from the Llanelli direction by Arthur, who found it in his shoe.

7 WESTERN RIVERS
The Teifi and Tywi

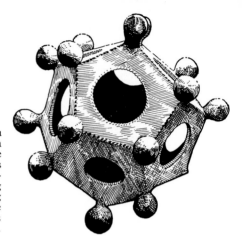

Figure 29. Carmarthen (Area 37): a bronze dodecahedron from the Roman town. The graded series of twelve holes may have served as a workshop gauge, or in opposing pairs as a simple surveying instrument; but it may be simply a candlestick. Scale 1:2 *Society of Antiquaries, London.*

THE UPPER TYWI
AREA 36

61 km (38 miles)
Carmarthenshire CM
Map 146; 1″ 140; 2½″ SN *62–64, 72–74*

The market towns of Llandeilo and Llandovery have both grown up at focal points of modern communications, which are forced to follow the valleys. It is difficult to plan a purposeful tour of archaeological sites without retracing one's route occasionally. Llandovery is more centrally placed for this area, but Llandeilo may be preferred.

The River Tywi (anglicised to Towy) rises well to the N. in the Cambrian Mountains. Its upper reaches, and those of the Cothi, cut through moorland where the only traces of prehistory are isolated Bronze Age cairns. The Iron Age settlement pattern, based on a cattle economy, seems to have been centred on large hillforts in the broader parts of the valley. The Roman military system of roads and forts made use of the main valley, but took to the high ground for vital links with other valleys, including the Cothi and its important gold-mining establishment.

Little can be seen of the Roman fort at *Llandovery (770 352)*, but excavation has shown it to have been built soon after the mid I century in the conquest campaign, later reduced from 2.5 ha to half size, and abandoned before A.D. 200. The *Roman road* to the S.W. (Fig. 12) can be identified at several places (e.g. *140 329, 725 322, 690 295, 663 274*).

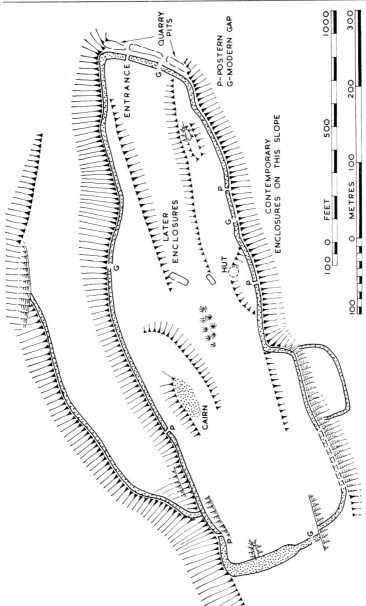

Figure 30. Carn Goch (Area 36): one of the largest stone-built hillforts of South Wales. *After A. H. A. Hogg.*

At the last it is recognisable as an *agger* 14 m wide in a field N. of the road fork. At *Llys Brychan* (*705 255*) the remains of a villa of some prosperity, dating from *c.* A.D. 200 to the IV century, indicate that civil settlement of the standard Roman colonial pattern extended at least this far from the south coastal plain.

Waun Pwtlyn Long Cairn   *709 260* CM

The mound is 40 m long but only half as wide, and is preserved to a height of 2 m, so that it is plainly in view from the road on the W. It is set in the valley bottom, and is thus comparable in size and position to several of the Severn-Cotswold tombs of Brecknock and Glamorgan, though no trace of a chamber is visible.

Carn Goch Hillfort
Fig. 30; *PEW* p. 136   *691 243* CM

The stone rampart which encloses an area of 10 ha at the top of the ridge is much ruined, but visible detail includes four postern gates and a larger gap for the main entrance at the N.E. end, all lined with upright slabs. The defence across the S.W. end is at least 20 m thick. There is only one hut platform inside, in contrast to the stone forts of north Wales. **Gaer Fach** (*685 242*) is a hillfort of about one-sixth the size, on the ridge to the W. It has only a weak dry-stone rampart, double in places. Its relationship to the larger fort is uncertain. A third at **Llwyn Du** (*679 244*) differs from both in its dependence on natural defences on one side, and multiple ramparts at the S.W. All three may represent a sequence occasioned by changing requirements and fashions in fortification.

Also nearby stands **Sythfaen Llwyn-du** (*675 244*), a stone nearly 3 m high, on which traces of deliberate shaping have been seen by some. Returning towards Llanwrda one passes **Carreg Fawr** (*695 293*) at the roadside. Though equally tall it is considerably less slender than the last, but it remains hard to judge the truth of the tradition that it is a memorial to the Battle of Bosworth rather than a Bronze Age burial marker.

By taking the A482 from Llanwrda the route of the Roman road from Llandovery north-westward can be picked up at **Aber Bowlan** (*698 388*). Here it descends 100 m in a distance of 500 m by means of a typically well engineered zigzag.

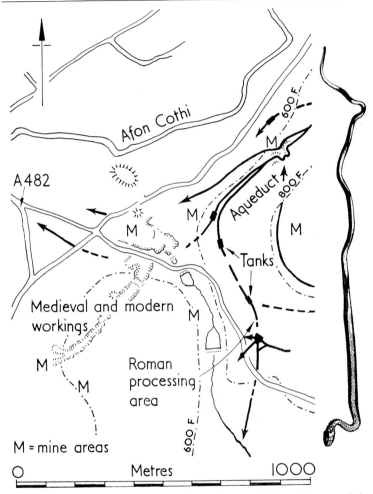

Figure 31. Dolaucothi Gold Mines (Area 36): map of the mining area (*after G. B. D. Jones*); and *right* a snake of solid gold, originally a bracelet, from a contemporary hoard. Scale 1:2. *British Museum.*

Dolaucothi Roman Gold Mines

Fig. 31; *INV* No. 113   *665 403* CM

A thorough investigation of the area is in progress, and has already proved the Roman date of the water tanks and channels on the hillside. The rocky slope where they end has also been shown to be the site of the final processing. The actual mines of Roman date are not easy to find among the medieval and recent exploitations. An aqueduct, however, can be traced up the Cothi valley for 11 km by following the contours, and another for 6 km up the parallel valley of the Annell, though they have been obliterated over several stretches. The water was also used in sudden releases for the technique of 'hushing' at places along the valley where gold-bearing rock was exposed on the hillside below the aqueduct. The prosperity arising from the mining can be judged from the hoard of precious objects found locally (Fig. 31). Though the actual engineering involved was probably under the supervision of military experts, commercial control would have been a civilian affair. Neither military nor civil living quarters have been positively identified, but the village of Pumpsaint has begun to yield traces of a fort. Explanatory pamphlets can be obtained at the Cothi Arms.

| THE LOWER TYWI | 45 km (28 miles) |
| AREA 37 | Carmarthenshire CM |

Map 149, 159; 1″ 139, 140, 151; 2½″ SN *31, 32, 41, 42, 52*

Carmarthen is the natural choice as a base from which adjacent areas also can be visited with ease. It is a thriving commercial and administrative centre, which serves the whole of west Wales beyond the Tywi.

The lower reaches of the Tywi also formed a natural boundary to the territory which was occupied by the Demetae at the Roman conquest, and Carmarthen was their tribal capital, at the root of west Wales. There is a marked difference in the hillforts in each direction, with a predominance of the smaller hillslope and inland promontory types westward, while the forts of the valley are of the larger refuge type, already seen in Area 36.

Twlc y Filiast Cromlech
PEW p. 50
335 162 CM
Sited by a brook in a small, steep-sided valley, the small trapezoid

chamber recalls the portal dolmen form seen at Dyffryn (Area 19). An antechamber and a small ritual pit were found in recent excavations, and an oval cairn 18 m long by 9 m was traced. In the same triangle between the Rivers Tywi and Taf are several Bronze Age standing stones; one at *Maesgwyn* (*360 136*) was found on excavation to have only 0.3 m of its 2.75 m height in the ground, resting on a prepared bed of clay. A shallow pit in front contained charcoal and some flint flakes.

Iron Age forts in the same district include **Castell Cogan** (*327 140*), partly bivallate, the inner bank being particularly strong. At *Llanstephan Castle* (*351 101*) a semicircular bank and ditch round the medieval remains seems to be prehistoric in origin. **Pen y Gaer** (*307 193*) is a small hilltop site with concentric defences, and an annexe to the W.

Castell y Gaer
INV No. 629   *343 195* CM
An oval hilltop enclosure of 2 ha with two simple entrances through a rampart up to 3 m high. A small inner enclosure in the N.E. part could be a Roman period adaptation of a pre-Roman fort.

Meini Gwyn
INV No. 512   *459 261* CM
Two stones almost 3 m high stand 100 m apart. A third lies prostrate 20 m further E. A stone of similar size is *Llech Ciste* (*514 283*), which has two smaller stones at equal spacing (3.5 m) each side, and a fourth 16 m further to the S.E. Both groups are assumed to be Bronze Age burial markers.

Merlin's Hill
                                                          455 215 CM
Surprisingly only recently discovered, this 4 ha hillfort has a single massive rampart, with an entrance in the N.E. corner strongly defended by an inturn and a formidable outwork.

Carmarthen Roman Fort and Town
Fig. 32; *RFW* p. 73   *415 202* CM
Roman settlement has been recognised for very many years, but evidence from finds has not been adequately collated. Now a full investigation is under way, and already excavation in the limited spaces available has put beyond doubt the position not only of the military fort of

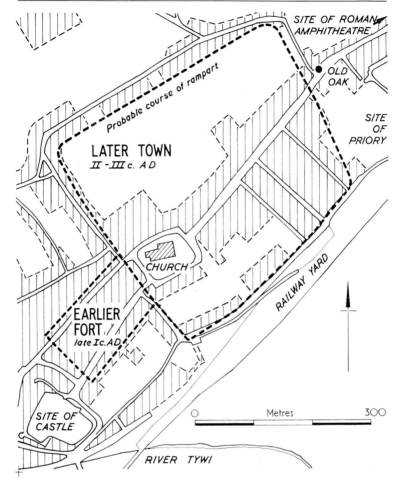

Figure 32. Roman Carmarthen (Area 37): the probable layout in the eastern part of the town. *After G. D. B. Jones.*

Moridunum (late I century A.D.), but also of the civil town which followed it (II–IV centuries), with timber buildings in the interior and even the refinement of an amphitheatre outside its E. gate. The sequence is historically significant as indicating early adaptation to Roman rule in Demetia (of which this was presumably the capital) as compared with

Silurian territory (see Area 29). The fort was primarily established as the S.W. corner of the military framework of roads and forts (Fig. 12), but a peaceful pattern of commerce and agriculture developed, in which sites like Cwmbrwyn (Area 40) assume a non-military role along with the civil town.

Carmarthen Museum

Quay St.   *412 198* CM

Started as the collection of the Carmarthenshire Antiquarian Society, and now the responsibility of the County Council, it has been housed in conditions (soon to be remedied) that do little justice to its importance as the repository of key material, not only from the town but from the countryside well beyond the county boundary. In the museum are six early Christian inscribed stones of the V–VI century. One commemorating 'Bivadus, son of Bodibeva' has an ogam repetition of the Latin, as also has that of 'Voteporix, the Protector', a local chieftain with a hereditary Roman title. On another (Fig. 33) a long inscription in bad verse praises 'Paulinus, preserver of the Faith, constant lover of his country, the devoted champion of righteousness'. St. David's tutor of that name died in the mid VI century.

Figure 33. Carmarthen Museum (Area 37): a memorial stone of the VI century. Scale 1:10. *After V. E. Nash-Williams.*

THE UPPER TEIFI
AREA 38

80 km (50 miles)
Cardiganshire CD, Carmarthenshire CM
Map 146; 1″ 127, 139, 140; 2½″ SN *45, 53–55, 64–66, 75, 76*

Lampeter is a small market town with its own university college, and is well placed for routes along the Teifi valley and into the hills on either side. Aberaeron and Tregaron have some accommodation also, and Tregaron is a pony-trekking centre for those who care to try reaching the more remote moorland sites on horseback.

Cardiganshire has been little explored archaeologically, but even when due allowance is made for that, the Upper Teifi area seems to have been sparsely populated in antiquity. Between the Teifi and the sea are small fortified settlements on hillslopes and promontories, native Iron Age sites possibly spanning the Roman conquest. The mountain range to the S.E., shared by Area 36, must have been a great attraction in drier Bronze Age times for the hunters and pastoralists whose cairns are their only witness. Tregaron Bog lies between as an impassable barrier.

Cribyn Gaer   *520 509* CD

A small but strongly defended hillfort. The main bank and ditch round the raised end of a ridge are supplemented by two extra ramparts on the S.E. **Castell Moeddyn** (*485 520*) is somewhat similarly sited.

Cwm Castell (*469 554*) is a small hillfort depending partly on the natural strength of its position, but with its bank and ditch doubled on the S. **Coedparc Gaer** (*588 514*), on a spur overlooked by higher ground to the N.E., has a single line of defence arranged to form an overlapping entrance.

Evidence of the Roman period in the Teifi valley is confined to the military network of roads and forts. Bremia at *Llanio* (*644 564*) is typically sited in the flood plain on a low knoll. The exact position has only recently been verified, and a bath house nearby testifies to an establishment of some permanence, presumably as a posting-station for policing activities during the Occupation. The road northwards (Fig. 12) is still followed by modern lanes, but at **Blaenyresgair** (*645 655*) it is clearly seen to veer E. of the A485 towards Trawscoed (Area 22).

Castell Fflemish   *654 632* CD

A small summit is fortified with two widely spaced banks. This is one of several sites to which an Iron Age date is only tentatively given, with early medieval as the alternative. The bivallate fort at **Sunnyhill Wood** (*687 602*), on the other hand, is a strongly defended inland promontory fort of more typical Iron Age character. The fort on **Pen y Bannau** (*742 669*), 8 km to the N.E., which can be approached from Strata Florida Abbey, has only one rampart owing to the natural strength of its position on a narrow ridge, but two extra banks give added defence to the entrance at the N. end.

Sites to be reached only on foot or on horseback in the mountains E. of Tregaron include a small hillfort, *Castell Rhyfel* (*732 599*), and Bronze Age *cairns* at five locations within 3 km of it, all shown on the o.s. 1″ map. For motorists a mountain road passes near to others at *669 531, 685 514, 694 514, 643 476* and *648 482*. The last two are on either side of a section of the **Roman road** from Dolaucothi (Area 36) to Bremia.

Hirfaen Gwyddog
INV No. 611   *624 464* CM
4.5 m high and nearly as much in girth, it has been used as a marker for the county boundary, but may have been set up originally in prehistoric times.

Mynydd Llanybyther Alignment
INV No. 604   *549 395* CM
At least 18 stones have been counted, set in an almost exactly east–west alignment. The highest measure nearly 1 m, but the smallest barely penetrate the grass, so that many of the larger gaps (up to 110 m) may have been filled at a smaller spacing. The closest are 13 m apart. Stone alignments are rare in Wales, and their purpose is hard to assess except in general terms as Bronze Age ceremonial settings. A good group of four cairns nearby is **Crugiau Edryd** (*535 395*), set in line about 15 m apart.

THE LOWER TEIFI   61 km (38 miles)
AREA 39   Cardiganshire CD, Carmarthenshire CM
                   Map 145; 1″ 139; 2½″ SN *24, 25, 33–35, 43, 44*

The tourist attractions of the south Cardigan Bay coast are being greatly developed, so that accommodation should be no problem at any time of the year, but Newcastle Emlyn should be tried for its central position in this area.

The lower reaches of the Teifi, famous for its fishing and its wicker-work coracles, continue from Area 38 the separation of the coastal ridge from the inland mountain spine, which runs on westwards to Pembrokeshire, well covered with Bronze Age burial mounds. The small fortified settlements N. of the river can be classed as Iron Age only in the broadest sense, though two of them have provided decorated bronze objects which indicate a thriving La Tène art tradition.

Castell Nadolig
Fig. 34   *298 504* CD

A good example of a fortified site depending on the depth of its defences rather than on a strong position. The two concentric banks are some 60 m apart, thus providing a space which is likely to have served for penning the stock on which the economy depended. The curvilinear decoration on the two bronze 'spoons' found here tells of immigrant metalworkers from south-west England, where the same type of fortification is found.

Three small forts which make good use of natural strength of position

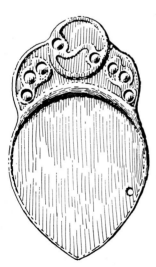

Figure 34. Castell Nadolig (Area 39): one of a pair of bronze 'spoons' with Celtic decoration. Scale 1:2. *National Museum of Wales.*

Figure 35. Pencoedfoel (Area 39): one half of a bronze collar found in the Iron Age fort. Scale 1:2. *National Museum of Wales.*

are **Castell Blaen Igau** (*341 506*), **Caerau, Blaenbarre** (*360 494*) and **Dinas Cerdin** (*386 470*), the last two having double ramparts where the ground requires them. **Pencoedfoel** (*425 428*) is larger, with a defensive depth of 12 m in its bank, ditch and counterscarp bank. The half of a bronze collar found here (Fig. 35) is clearly of pre-Roman Celtic type, perhaps as early as 200 B.C.

Craig Gwrtheyrn
INV No. 393   *433 403* CM
In an imposing position S. of the Teifi, with a strong stone-built defence following the contours. Two further banks create a barbican at the S.W. entrance, which is further protected by a small area of *chevaux-de-frise*, a feature of distinctly foreign origin. Further down the valley, on a low-lying promontory at *Henllan* (*358 402*), a small fort was excavated before its destruction. The defensive technique suggested Iron Age B affinity for a small group of cattle farmers penetrating the region from the sea, but certainty is difficult in the absence of pottery or other clearly datable finds.

The hills S.W. of Newcastle Emlyn are notable for the large number of Bronze Age cairns which have survived. Several lie near the roads, and can be seen from them (a selection is given here, but others can be found from o.s. maps, to a total of about 40):

Crugiau (*410 360*), three in line. **Carn Wern** (*359 342*), one of ten on this east–west ridge. **Crug Disgwylfa** (*320 318*), disturbed by the road. **Crug Ieuan** (*312 312*), recently cut in two by the road. See Area 40 also.

Clawdd Mawr
INV No. 100   *377 336* CM
A cross-ridge dyke about 3 km long, best seen where it follows a minor north–south ridge for 1 km along the A484. It faces E., the ditch on that side being well preserved in places, and was probably constructed as a territorial boundary in the XI century A.D.

Cerrig Llwydion
PEW p. 49   *374 326* CM
A large flat stone is in position on three uprights. Further slabs standing cross-wise to the modern wall show this to have been a megalithic tomb of the segmented cist variety seen also at Trefignath (Area 1), but no forecourt survives to support the apparent connection with the Irish court cairns.

8 SOUTH-WEST WALES
Pembrokeshire

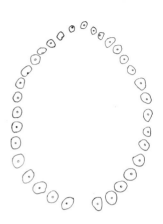

Figure 36. Nab Head (Area 44): a number of tiny pebbles of shale, pierced presumably for use as ornaments, found at a mesolithic settlement site on the cliff top. Scale 1:3. *In Carmarthen Museum.*

THE CARMARTHENSHIRE TAF   66 km (41 miles)

AREA 40   Carmarthenshire CM, Pembrokeshire PE

Map 158; 1″ 139, 152; 2½″ SN *11, 12, 20–22*

The Taf and its tributaries dissect the country immediately W. of Carmarthen into several parallel ridges, rooted in the mountain spine that joins central Wales to Mynydd Preseli. A barrier of hills dominates Carmarthen Bay on the S., turning the river westward in a broad vale with limited crossing points. This is a region through which many travellers pass, bound for the holiday coastline. Accommodation of the humbler kind is not hard to find in Narberth, Laugharne or St. Clears, with Carmarthen, Tenby and Haverfordwest as larger alternatives within easy reach of the sites to be visited.

The direct route from St. Clears to the coast passes the excavated site at *Cwmbrwyn* (Fig. 37; *254 122*), originally interpreted as 'a small military outpost designed to guard forward lines of communication' during the II–IV centuries A.D. The more recent view that the Roman occupation of Demetic territory was non-military would make this a farmhouse fortified for individual security. A similar site was excavated at *Trelissey* (*174 078*) 9 km to the S.W.

A longer route leads from Laugharne past the limestone projection of *Coygan Hill* (*284 092*; *COY*) which attracted occupation in most periods of prehistory. From *Coygan Cave* high on the S.E. side came the only two palaeolithic hand-axes from a stratified context in Wales. During excavation of the hillfort which crowns the summit (soon to be

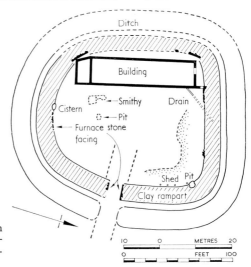

Figure 37. Cwmbrwyn (Area 40): a native homestead of the Roman period. *After J. Ward.*

quarried away) both mesolithic and neolithic material came to light, the latter being carbon-dated to *c.* 3000 B.C. The first Iron Age settlement, within the VIII–II centuries B.C., was undefended and was based on mixed farming. The mainly pastoral group who followed built a strong rampart to enclose the promontory. The final phase was an undefended homestead of the late III century A.D., in which a coin-hoard testifies to the activities of a group of counterfeiters.

Gilman Camp
INV No. 701   *228 076* CM
Fortification of two periods is represented by a walled ringwork apparently preceding a small promontory fort. A cross-bank divides the latter into two enclosures, the S. one having its own entrance while the N. one had a simple gap in the massive main defence.

Pendine Head Burial Chambers
PCT p. 206   *222 075* PE
Four small chambered cairns lie in line on a terrace 60 m above the sea. From S. to N. the first is a closed rectangular chamber in an oval mound. 40 m away is an irregular pentagonal chamber in a round cairn. After 75 m is a collection of stones seen by some as the site of a third—the nearby 'Druid's Altar' is a natural rock. The fourth at the same

M

distance again is the best preserved, with its capstone in place. A natural slab has been underpinned to form a rectangular chamber 2.1 m by 1.4 m partly cut into the ground, approached by a short passage from the edge of its round cairn. It thus belongs, together with its more ruined neighbours, to the passage grave tradition, though at an almost final stage of devolution from the primary idea as seen at Barclodiad y Gawres (Area 1).

Llanddewi Gaer
INV No. 420   *144 160* PE

Occupies the edge of a scarp facing S.E., with a triple bank system across the more level ground on the N.W. The S.W. side of the enclosure has been virtually levelled, but the original entrance is visible at the N.

Caerau Gaer
INV No. 421   *139 161* PE

On a rounded spur at about the same level as the last, but without the same naturally strong position. It is completely encircled by a single bank and ditch, with traces of an outwork for extra defence on the saddle to the N.E. The gap on the N.E. is more likely to be the original entrance than that on the W.

Meini Gwyr Circle
SCW p. 141   *142 266* CM

On the broad ridge which constitutes part of the likely route for the Stonehenge 'bluestones' (see Area 41); only two remain of the 17 stones which once made up the embanked circle. Excavation revealed a passage-like entrance on the W. and suggested an Early Bronze Age date. Note a good **cairn circle** at *145 270.*

Dolwilym Burial Chamber
PCT p. 206   *170 256* CM

Variously known as Bwrdd Arthur and Gwalyfiliast, this cromlech was said in 1872 to have been covered by a barrow with a surrounding circle of 32 stones, but no trace remains of either feature, and only four upright stones still support the capstone.

The ridge to the east of the Taf carries many examples of Bronze Age burial mounds in a series reaching 12 km N.N.E. from **Cross-hands** (*195 228*) and continued in Area 39. As is usual, some are badly damaged by ploughing and may be covered by crops, but a careful choice of those marked on the 1″ map will ensure a fair sampling on the return route to St. Clears. In general they are between 20 and 30 m in diameter and up to 2 m high, the burial places of the nomadic, pastoral people who followed the neolithic settlement phase.

PRESELI NORTH   56 km (35 miles)
AREA 41   Pembrokeshire PE
                    Map 145, 157; 1″ 138, 139; 2½″ SM *93*, SN *03, 04, 13, 14*

The popular holiday coast of north Pembrokeshire provides a good choice of places to stay, though they may need searching out. Newport is the natural centre for this area, though Fishguard or Cardigan may be preferred.

The northern foothills of Mynydd Preseli and the Nevern valley form a unit of land reasonably attractive for agricultural settlement. Prehistoric recognition of this is attested for the Neolithic period by communal megalithic tombs, and for Iron Age times by hillforts of a size suitable for tribal refuge in addition to the smaller defended settlements. The Preseli ridge itself forms a focus of late neolithic and Bronze Age activity.

Carreg Coetan Arthur
PCT p. 199   *059 393* PE
The sloping capstone and the two highest stones of the four remaining uprights give an impression recalling Irish portal dolmens. The vestigial mound and outlying stones give no further information. The chamber at **Trelyffant** (*082 425*) is ill defined, but the upper surface of its capstone bears 22 cupmarks. (*Cf.* Bachwen, Area 5.)

Nevern Memorial Stones
ECMW Nos. 353, 354, 360   *083 401* PE
The great cross of *c.* A.D. 1000 standing 4 m high in the churchyard, covered with panels of all kinds of interlaced decoration, is akin to the Carew Cross (Area 45). Its inscriptions are obscure, but those in Latin and ogam on two pillar stones of *c.* A.D. 500 clearly commemorate Maglicunus, son of Clutorius, and Vitalianus Emeretos.

Plate 27. Foel Trigarn (Area 41): Bronze Age cairns crowning an Iron Age fort on the Preseli Mountains. *Photo: J. K. S. St. Joseph.*

Foel Trigarn

Pl. 27; *PEW* p. 142   *158 336* PE

The main inner enclosure at the summit (about 1.2 ha) has two further enclosures (both about 0.8 ha) built on the N. and W. slopes. Each is defended by a single rampart of dry stone and earth with no ditch, and can only be presumed to be successive in date. Hut platforms are common in the inner two, and finds of beads and pottery range in date from Iron Age A to Roman. The three large Bronze Age cairns have been sadly mutilated. In view from Foel Trigarn is **Carn Alw** (*139 337*), a rocky knoll on the broad mountain slope, where outcrops have been joined by a stone-faced bank to make an Iron Age fort. A notable feature is the area of *chevaux-de-frise* on the W., through which a stone-lined route leads to the entrance.

The outcrops of **Carn Meini** (*14 32*) on the skyline to the S.W. are partly composed of a distinctive blue-grey dolerite with large white spots, confirmed in 1923 by petrological examination as one of the rock-types found in the earliest stone element of Stonehenge. It weathers down in a columnar form that obviated quarrying; suitable shapes were selected, along with some of other material, including an unspotted form of the dolerite and rhyolites possibly from Carn Alw. The method of transport and the route used have been thoroughly investigated, being most probably a combination of sledging overland on rollers (starting down the ridge followed by the A478), and rafts taken round the coast (embarking at the head of the tidal eastern branch of the Cleddau). The unsolved questions include the reason for this massive effort, which could lie in the known superiority of the same spotted dolerite as raw material for the neolithic axe trade.

Pentre Ifan
Fig. 38; *PCT* p. 199   *099 370* PE
This chambered tomb has a clear link, in its crescentic façade, high portal and slightly tapering cairn, with the court cairns of north Ireland and south-west Scotland. A level floor was made by cutting into the hillside, and the chamber sides were completed with dry walling, with a false blocking stone built into the entrance. The north–south orientation of the cairn is unusual, and it contains in its length of over 36 m alignments of stones and ritual pits whose purpose can only be guessed. Fully excavated and conserved by the State, open always without charge. A pamphlet is available.

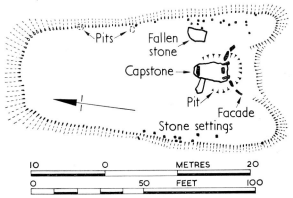

Figure 38. Pentre Ifan (Area 41): a neolithic chambered long cairn with Irish affinities. *After H.M.S.O. Guide, Crown Copyright.*

Bedd-yr-Afanc

PCT p. 203   *108 345* PE
The gallery form of the chamber, 11.4 m long, points to an isolated connection with southern Ireland. Excavation produced no conclusive dating evidence.

Carn Ingli   *063 372* PE

The rocky end of the broad moorland behind Newport has been turned into a strong fort by ramparts which join the crags, and loop far down the slope to the S.E. to enclose an extensive series of terraces. Here would have been a good refuge for an agricultural population depending to a large extent on a cattle-raising economy. The same applies to **Carn Ffoi** (*049 379*) on a smaller scale.

Also in the coastal hills are several Bronze Age stones, among which **Garreg Hir** (*064 351*), about 3 m in height and girth, and **Bedd Morris** (*037 365*), 2.3 m high, are close to lanes. *Ty Meini* (*995 376*) and the *Lady Stone* (*008 387*) are similar to the last in height.

Parc y Meirw   *998 358* PE

Four of the eight stones in this alignment are still standing, in a length of 40 m, the tallest being about 2.5 m high.

Cerrig y Gof

PCT p. 199   *037 389* PE
Five rectangular chambers, of which only one retains its capstone, are set radially in a round cairn, an arrangement that seems to be a local development under Bronze Age influence, without clear parallel in the Irish Sea area. Excavation *c.* 1800 produced charcoal, undefined pottery, bones and 'a quantity of black sea pebbles'.

THE CLEDDAU   61 km (38 miles)
AREA 42   Pembrokeshire PE
            Map 158; 1″ 138, 139; 2½″ SM *91, 92,* SN *01, 02, 12*

Haverfordwest, the administrative and market town of south Pembrokeshire, is acquiring a new importance in relation to the many holiday villages which are being developed around the coast. Archaeological sightseers here can be assured of all that they may require.

The eastern and western heads of Milford Haven are the outlets of the Cleddy Ddu and Cleddy Wen respectively. Both rise in the Preseli range and descend through land which becomes more hospitable for cultivation towards the S. and W. The higher ground is noticeably rich in Bronze Age stone monuments, while the lower ground is similar to the Milford Peninsula (Area 44) with its small Iron Age fortified settlements. *Walesland Rath* (*916 173*) has proved an important type site of the latter during its total excavation in advance of destruction, with pre-Roman occupation of the I century A.D. overlaid by Romano-British levels of the late III century.

Poll Carn   *952 245* PE

Only a single bank and ditch defend this rocky spur on the N. and S., but it is noteworthy for the *chevaux-de-frise* of pitched boulders fronting it on the E. as a deterrent to attack. (*Cf.* Carn Alw, Area 41.)

Between Wolf's Castle and Treffgarne the western branch of the Cleddau breaks dramatically through a prominent ridge on which are several prominent barrows. Those near the B4330 include a group on **Plumstone Mountain** (*917 234*).

Carn Turne
Pl. 28; *PCT* p. 200   *979 272* PE

Though the capstone of this chambered tomb has collapsed with its supporters, the V-shaped forecourt fronting it is a feature which connects it at least with the general western family of long cairns. The boulders lying around and behind the chamber are basically the remnants of a ridge of outcrop which could have been used as the foundation of such a cairn.

On the S.E. side of B4329 are more outliers of the Bronze Age sites of eastern Preseli (see Areas 40 and 41). The **Dyffryn Stones** (*059 285*) are a circle of 13, 20 m in diameter. The **Budloy Stone** (*065 285*) is supposedly tooled on its W. side. Two monoliths stand 2 m high and 40 m apart at **Cornel Bach** (*082 280*) while the **Parcytywod Stone** (*088 278*) is taller at 2.6 m and has a flat slab at its base.

Gors Fawr Circle
SCW p. 145   *134 294* PE

The 16 remaining stones, none of which is much over 1 m high, are

Plate 28. Carn Turne (Area 42): a little-known megalithic tomb with V-shaped forecourt.

spaced from 2.4 to 5.2 m apart in a circle of about 22 m diameter, but are not incorporated in a bank, as at Meini Gwyr (Area 40). The two larger stones to the N.E. may be related as outliers.

The return to Haverfordwest can be made by way of three inland fortifications. **Castell Rhyd-y-brwyn** (*066 223*) is strongly sited on a small spur at the S. end of a broad ridge. The main bank and two outer banks are well preserved on the N. and W. Recent excavations at *Knock Rath* (*038 218*), a subrectangular site with stone-revetted bank within a deep rock-cut ditch, revealed Romano-British occupation, as also at *Merryborough Camp* (*008 173*), now levelled.

Haverfordwest Museum
The Castle   *953 157* PE
Pembrokeshire for many years lacked a County Museum, though the need was admirably fulfilled on a more restricted basis by the private museum at Tenby. Many finds, however, which should have remained in the county found their way to Carmarthen and elsewhere. Now the County Council has set things to rights by converting the former jail

in Haverfordwest Castle for this purpose with full-time officers in charge. For obvious reasons the collection is scanty—at least for pre-history—but one may hope for some improvement, whether from new discoveries or by a negotiated transfer of material.

THE ST. DAVIDS PENINSULA
AREA 43

66 km (41 miles)
Pembrokeshire PE
Map 157; 1″ 138; 2½″ SM *72, 82, 83, 93*

The ancient ecclesiastical centre of St. Davids is small, but accommodation can be found here and in the holiday village of Solva. Fishguard is also within easy reach. There is a useful information centre of the Pembrokeshire National Park at St. Davids.

Though there are several small promontory and other forts to compare with those of south Pembrokeshire (Areas 44, 45), it is the abundance of

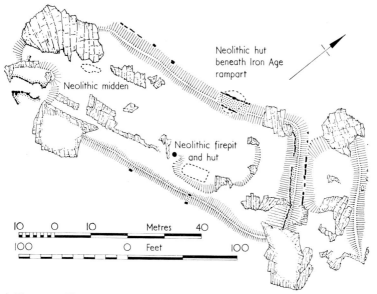

Figure 39. Clegyr Boia (Area 43): a neolithic dwelling site on a rocky knoll, fortified 2,000 years later by Iron Age settlers. *After A. Williams.*

megalithic remains that is the conspicuous feature here in the north of the county, which firmly faces the Irish Sea (along with Area 41) and has partaken of the neolithic cultural unity of that province.

Clegyr Boia
Fig. 39; *PEW* p. 57   *737 252* PE
The rocky summit of a small hill has been enclosed by ramparts joining outcrops to form a secure Iron Age dwelling site, for which precise dating evidence was lacking in excavation. Important neolithic remains included the substantial rectangular house of a group of cattle farmers, whose pottery indicates an Irish connection in the third millennium B.C.

Carn Llidi
PCT p. 202   *735 279* PE
Two sub-megalithic chambers (*cf.* Carn Wnda below), with slabs over rock-cut pits, only partly supported by orthostats, lie together on the N. slope beneath the signal station. There are no certain traces of a covering mound. 1 km further W., however, **Coetan Arthur** (*725 280*) has a round barrow, and a possible passage leading to the collapsed chamber.

Close by also is **Clawdd y Milwyr** (*722 279*), an Iron Age promontory fort with a setting of upright slabs defining the approach to the entrance. There are traces of huts within, and an extensive system of enclosures outside, presumably contemporary. Excavation finds (in Tenby Museum) indicate a final pre-Roman date.

Carreg Samson, Longhouse
PCT p. 201   *848 335* PE
Three of the seven uprights of the polygonal chamber support the large capstone, but it lacks a cairn or other distinctive features. Excavation has shown that the entrance was at the N.W. corner through a passage, and that the uprights are based in the edge of a single large pit. In State care, open always without charge. *Ffyst Samson* (*906 349*) is less complete, with only two broad supporters beneath its capstone.

Garn Fawr
INV No. 554   *896 388* PE
The dry-stone rampart construction seen in the forts of Area 41 is repeated in the triple widely spaced defences, probably of several periods. The mutilated entrance works look towards a smaller fort on

Garn Fechan 200 m to the E. (*900 389*). **Dinas Mawr** (*887 387*) is a well sited promontory fort, with central entrances through two banks across its narrow isthmus.

Carn Wnda
PCT p. 200   *932 392* PE
A good example of the sub-megalithic type of burial chamber, in which the capstone is not entirely supported by upright stones (two here), but rests partly on the edge of a rock-cut pit. Early excavation revealed a cremation burial in an urn of unspecified type. The three chambers at **Carn Wen** (*948 390*), each in its own round cairn, are also partly rock-cut, the southernmost being the best preserved. A more orthodox chamber with a faint mound at **Penrhiw** (*942 390*) has three upright slabs in a rectangular arrangement.

Rhos y Clegryn
                                                         913 354 PE
A fine monolith 2.75 m high stands by a flattened round cairn. Current excavations have revealed neolithic habitation preceding, and probably quite unconnected with, the later monuments. The return route to St. Davids passes **Maen Dewi** (*776 275*), another accessible *maenhir*, 2.4 m high.

St. Davids Cathedral
ECMW Nos. 373–383   *752 254* PE
There are a dozen or so inscribed and decorated stones at the Cathedral, including wheel-crosses of the IX and X centuries, either carved in relief on rough slabs or fully sculptured.

THE MILFORD PENINSULA   56 km (35 miles)
AREA 44   Pembrokeshire PE
           Map 157; 1″ 151; 2½″ SM 70, 71, 80, 81, 90, 91

As for Area 42, Haverfordwest is the best starting point. Milford Haven is more concerned with the oil trade and other distractions, but Dale and Broadhaven are just two of several tourist-conscious villages where a short stay is recommended.

The western branch of the Cleddau (Cleddy Wen) is tidal as far as Haverfordwest, the lowest point at which it can be crossed by road. The N. side of Milford Haven is thus a peninsula rooted in the hinterland of St. Brides Bay. Like the Tenby Peninsula (Area 45) it has few sites other than those which fall into the dual pattern of inland and coastal Iron Age settlement.

The Hanging Stone, Burton
PCT p. 202   *972 082* PE

A megalithic burial chamber standing in isolation as the best-preserved example of a cromlech in south Pembrokeshire, though somewhat encumbered by field walls. A second capstone and two uprights in the hedge could have been part of a passage leading to the simple main chamber, but in the absence of a mound its classification remains uncertain.

The route westward passes two constrasting inland Iron Age forts. At **Thornton Rath** (*905 079*) a promontory has been used to advantage, with some scarping of its natural slopes, and a semicircular double line of defence on the more level ground. At **Capeston Rath** (*867 094*) only a short stretch of natural scarp has been used, resulting in an almost complete ring of banks. The word Rath is commonly used in Pembrokeshire in naming fortifications of all types well into medieval times, and does not have the restricted meaning familiar in Ireland.

The Long Stone, Mabesgate   *828 076* PE

Aptly named, since it is the tallest in the county, leaving little doubt that it marks the site of a burial rather than being a late 'cattle rubbing-stone', as many of the shorter isolated stones must be.

Like the south coast of the Tenby Peninsula (Area 45), the promontories beyond Dale and Marloes lie right in the western seaway. The whole coast-line is worth covering on foot, but four of its characteristic cliff-top Iron Age sites deserve a special visit, involving less walking. **Great Castle Head** (*799 056*) has a complicated layout, resulting in great strength of defence in its series of banks and ditches. **Gateholm** (*770 073*) is a tidal island, and a ready-made stronghold. Rows of rectangular huts flanking a central 'street' have yielded pottery of Roman date, indicating continuity of settlement during the occupation of Wales. **Watery Bay Rath** (*768 079*) is very strongly defended, considering the small area of the interior. The innermost of its four banks is very striking. At the **Deer Park** (*758 090*) the whole western tip of

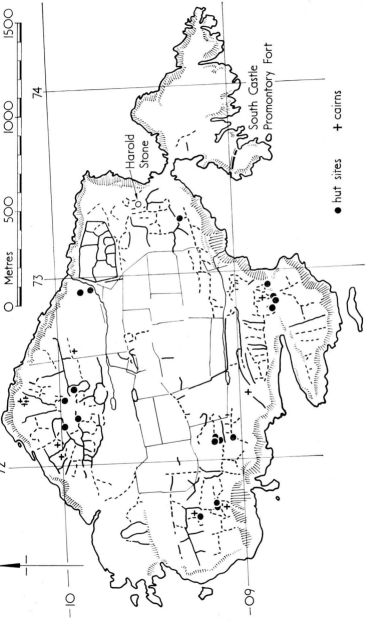

Figure 40. Skomer (Area 44): the huts and fields of Iron Age farmers, well preserved on an island sanctuary. *After W. F. Grimes.*

Harold Stone

South Castle
Promontory Fort

● hut sites   + cairns

O Metres   500   1000   1500

land, some 20 ha in area, has been cut off by a bank and ditch across the narrow neck at Martinshaven.

Huts and Fields on Skomer
Fig. 40   *72 09* etc. PE

Skokholm, which is famous as the resort of many thousands of sea birds, has no antiquities to offer, but its larger partner Skomer is closely covered by Iron Age huts and fields. The modern cultivation which has been pushed to the limit of the cliffs on the mainland has not impinged here. A few hours on the island will fully repay the time spent on the sea trip, which can be arranged at St. Davids. (Enquire at the National Park Information Centre.)

Each of the corners of the island has a fair sample of two types of field, walled all round on level ground or lynchetted on slopes. The huts are round or subrectangular, up to 7 m in diameter, some occurring in pairs. Their form and siting suggest a I century B.C. Cornish connection. The promontory fort at **South Castle** (*736 088*), with its single line of defence, is not necessarily a refuge contemporary with the settlements. Of the *cairns* marked on Fig. 40 among the fields some may result from ground clearance as distinct from burial.

Near the return route to Haverfordwest from Marloes are two further inland fortifications. **Romans Castle** (*895 106*) is an impressive hilltop site completely encircled by two banks, the inner being nearly 4 m high, with an inturned entrance at the S.W. **Denant** (*922 131*) by contrast is a promontory site with a single straight bank, ditch and counter-scarp bank, a type characteristic of the area around the Milford Haven inlets. **Haverfordwest Museum** (see Area 42).

THE TENBY PENINSULA   43 km (27 miles)
AREA 45   Pembrokeshire PE
     Map 158; 1″ 151, 152; 2½″ SM *80, 90,* SN *00, 10,* SR *89, 99,* SS *09, 19*

Tenby is a town where an archaeological holiday can be enjoyed in a truly historical atmosphere, along with the convenience of a well-provided resort. Though almost isolated from the rest of Pembrokeshire, the peninsula beyond Tenby has been open to the foreign influences reaching western Britain by sea in early times, for Milford Haven and sheltered bays on the south have always afforded a safe anchorage.

Penally Crosses
ECMW Nos. 363–4   *117 992* PE
A wheel-headed cross 1.5 m high in the church has rich interlaced carving, and the shaft of another shows beasts of Saxon derivation, indicating an early X century connection with Wessex.

Caldey Island
accessible by boat from Tenby   *14 96* PE
The monastic community now revived on Caldey welcomes visitors who share an interest in its heritage, which includes an ogam-inscribed *pillar stone* of *c.* A.D. 500 in the church (*141 963*), with an unusually fulsome VIII century inscription added. The prehistoric sites include *Nanna's Cave* (*145 969*), *Potter's Cave* (*143 971*) and the settlement at *Daylight Rock* (*149 966*), which have together produced a series of finds of primary importance in tracing the development of the Welsh Mesolithic. There is also pottery of both western neolithic and Peterborough type, and some of the earliest Iron Age material from Wales.

On the outward journey from Tenby along the south coast **Sampson Cross** (*965 965*) is one of three stones always associated, under the name Devil's Quoits, with *Harold's Stone*, at *967 958* and another monolith at *974 956*. Legend asserts that they 'dance the hay' together each year.

The coastal area beyond Bosherston has been subjected to military use, and much of it is permanently inaccessible, but three cliff-top forts offer a variety of Iron Age defensive features, contrasting in turn with a fourth site inland. **Buckspool Down Camp** (*954 934*) is a natural cliff-bound promontory dramatically cut off by a single bank on a bridge of rock 80 m long, with two outer banks added. There are two possible round huts within. **Crocksydam Camp** (*936 943*), occupying a wider angle in the cliffs, is also defended by a single bank, with a stone core at the W. end. A round stone hut lies within. **Flimston Camp** (*930 946*) is a natural promontory defended by two banks, with a third some 20 m further out. The entrance is clearly seen at the centre.

Inland lies **Merrion Camp** (*940 975*), its small interior encircled by very strong contour defences. The innermost is the best preserved of the four lines traceable on the level ground covering the entrance.

On one of the two ridges which run along the centre of the peninsula is the **Devil's Quoit** at *886 008* (unconnected with the three stones already noted) is a cromlech which has only one supporter in position under the capstone. No barrow can be traced.

Plate 29. Carew Cross (Area 45): late Celtic stone carving of excellent quality. 4 metres high. *National Monuments Record, Crown Copyright.*

Dry Burrows Tumuli

INV No. 334   *950 997* PE

A good group of seven burial mounds with outliers, the largest being some 3 m high and 35 m in diameter. Cremations were found in early excavations, with 'coal' in addition to charcoal.

In the dissected E. end of the ridges are two caves in which palaeolithic habitation has been found. *Hoyle's Mouth* (*111 003*), which is being opened up as a tourist attraction, produced recognisable Upper Aurignacian tools, while those from the *Longbury Bank Cave* or Little Hoyle (*112 001*) could not be so definitely assessed as could its early medieval occupation. Upper palaeolithic material found in *Priory Farm Cave* (*979 017*) near Pembroke can be assigned to the Creswellian culture, the precursor of the Mesolithic phase on Caldey Island.

Carew Cross

Pl. 29; *ECMW* No. 303   *046 037* PE

One of the largest (4 m high) and finest of the early Christian memorial stones of Wales. It is covered with frets and interlaces on the shaft, arranged in intricate panels on the faces. A small panel near the base commemorates Maredudd ap Edwin, a Welsh prince killed in A.D. 1035. In State care, accessible always without charge.

Tenby Museum

Castle Hill   *136 005* PE

Opened in 1878, and now affiliated to the National Museum of Wales, it is managed by a voluntary committee and depends on reasonable admission fees to maintain its high standard of display. There is important material from local excavations, including a restored bowl from Clegyr Boia (Area 43), and a special exhibit on the 'bluestone route' (Areas 40 to 42). From the Iron Age (Foel Trigarn, Area 41) the emphasis is on settlements, through the Roman period (Trelissey, Area 40) to early medieval times. Open every day, except Sunday and Friday afternoon from October to March.

N

BIBLIOGRAPHY

There is a great deal of specialist writing which is accessible only in libraries or by subscription, but most of the books listed here are reasonably obtainable. Abbreviations in *italic* type are those used in site descriptions.

General Surveys of Welsh Archaeology
Grimes, W. F. *The Prehistory of Wales* (2nd edn. 1951). Review of pre-Roman periods, with reference to National Museum collections.

Foster, I. Ll. and Alcock, L. (eds.) *Culture and Environment* (1963). Studies presented to Sir Cyril Fox, several on Welsh topics.

Foster, I. Ll. and Daniel, G. E. (eds.) *Prehistoric and Early Wales* (1965). Research and interpretation to 1960. *PEW*

Fox, Sir Cyril. *The Personality of Britain* (4th edn. 1959). Wales as part of Britain, with constant recourse to mapping.

Nash-Williams, V. E. (ed.) *A Hundred Years of Welsh Archaeology* (1948). Background to present knowledge of many important sites.

Regional Surveys
Watson, Katherine. *North Wales* (1965), and Houlder, C. H. and Manning, W. H. *South Wales* (1966). In a series for schools and adult education.

Site Studies
Powell, T. G. E. and Daniel, G. E. *Barclodiad y Gawres* (1956). Area 1. *BG*

Fox, Sir Cyril. *A find . . . from Llyn Cerrig Bach* (1946). Area 1. *LCB*

Gardner, W. and Savory, H. N. *Dinorben* (1964 and 1971). Area 9. *DIN*

Fox, Sir Cyril. *Offa's Dyke* (1955). Fieldwork 1926–34, including Wat's Dyke. Areas 11, 12, 13, 16, 25, 29. *OD*

Alcock, L. *Dinas Powis* (1963). Area 31. *DP*

Fox, Sir Cyril. *Life and Death in the Bronze Age* (1959). Area 32.

Wainwright, G. J. *Coygan Camp* (1967). Area 40. *COY*

All monuments in State guardianship (Department of the Environment, formerly Ministry of Public Building and Works) are described in official publications, obtainable from Government Bookshops (addresses on p. 28), but only a few have individual guides.

Regional Guides for *South Wales and Monmouthshire* (1969) and for *North Wales* (1969) describe all State-owned sites in their proper historical context. Both will shortly be superseded by a single *Illustrated Guide to the Ancient Monuments of Wales* and a shorter brochure.

Full Guides are available for the following sites:
The Ancient Monuments of Anglesey (1969); 17 sites in Areas 1 and 2. *Segontium Roman Fort* (1969); Area 5. *Caerwent Roman City* (1970); Area 29. *Caerleon Roman Amphitheatre and Prysg Field Barrack Buildings* (1970); Area 30. *Margam Stones Museum* (1967); Area 32.

Short pamphlets are available for the following:
Barclodiad y Gawres Burial Chamber; Area 1. *Capel Garmon Chambered Long Cairn*; Area 8. *Pillar of Eliseg*; Area 13. *Caerleon Roman Amphitheatre*; Area 30. *Tinkinswood and St. Lythan's Long Cairns*; Area 31. *Pentre-Ifan Burial Chamber*; Area 41.

Most of the primary sites in this book have a reference to one of the books listed below. Ideally the county *Inventories* should suffice, but only Anglesey, Caernarvonshire and Glamorgan are reliably up to date. Other general county surveys are rare, so that many references are to works dealing with periods or types of structure.

County Surveys

The *Inventories* of the Royal Commission on Ancient and Historical Monuments (H.M.S.O.).   *INV*

Lynch, Frances. *Prehistoric Anglesey* (1970). A new presentation, supplementing the Inventory with up-to-date research information.   *PA*

Davies, Ellis. *The Prehistoric and Roman Remains of Denbighshire* (1929) and . . . *Flintshire* (1949). One man's lifelong pursuit of the documentation of sites and finds in two counties.   *PRRD*
                                                                          PRRF

Bowen, E. G., and Gresham, C. A. *History of Merioneth*, Vol. I (1967). Renders *Inventory* virtually obsolete (to Norman conquest).   *HM*

Anglesey	1937	See also *PA* above	AN
Brecknock	(in preparation)		BR
Caernarvonshire,			
East I	1956		CA
Central II	1960		
West III	1964		
Cardiganshire	—	See *Handlist* below	CD
Carmarthenshire	1917		CM
Denbighshire	1914	See also *PRRD* above	DE
Flintshire	1912	See also *PRRF* above	FL
Glamorgan I	1974		GL
Merioneth	1921	See also *HM* above	ME
Monmouthshire	—	See *Handlist* below	MM
Montgomeryshire	1911		MY
Pembrokeshire	1925		PE
Radnorshire	1913		RA

Handlists of the Field Monuments of Wales are being produced by the Welsh Ancient Monuments Commission. Already available are *Cardiganshire* (1970) and *Monmouthshire* (1973), which list all known ancient structures with their grid references, but with no fine classification or description. Obtainable from H.M.S.O. (see p. 28).

Period and Typological Surveys

Piggott, S. *The Neolithic Cultures of the British Isles* (1954).

Daniel, G. E. *Prehistoric Chamber Tombs of England and Wales* (1950).   PCT

Powell, T. G. E. *et al. Megalithic Enquiries in the West of Britain* (1969). Chapters on Cotswold-Severn and North Wales tombs.

Grimes, W. F. 'The stone circles and related monuments of Wales'. A chapter in *Culture and Environment* (see General Surveys).   SCW

Ashbee, P. *The Bronze Age Round Barrow in Britain* (1960).

Thomas, Charles (ed.) *The Iron Age in the Irish Sea Province* (1972). Includes papers on coastal and border hillforts of Wales.

Fox, Sir Cyril. *Pattern and Purpose. Celtic Art in Britain* (1958).

Nash-Williams, V. E. *The Roman Frontier in Wales* (2nd edn. 1969). The military remains of the conquest and occupation.   RFW

Margary, I. D. *Roman Roads in Britain* (1967). Recent surveys
  have provided better alternatives to many general routes
  given here.
Rivet, A. L. F. (ed.) *The Roman Villa in Britain* (1969).
Nash-Williams, V. E. *The Early Christian Monuments of Wales   ECMW*
  (1950).

INDEXES

In the Subject Index certain entries have **reference letters** preceding the page numbers. These letters are used throughout the Sites Index to identify sites which belong to these more common types, which are too numerous to list in the entries of the Subject Index.

Deliberate omissions from this Index include common finds mentioned in the text as indicators of date for sites (e.g. pottery, coins); also names of all except the best-known persons mentioned in inscriptions.

Principal references to sites are shown in *italic*.

Subject Index

Sites Index